BE YOUR OWN COUNSELLOR

BE YOUR OWN COUNSELLOR

A STEP-BY-STEP

GUIDE TO

UNDERSTANDING

YOURSELF BETTER

SHEILA DAINOW

PIATKUS

*To Kate Williams, a creative,
challenging and supportive supervisor*

Acknowledgements

This is my chance to thank those people whose help in writing *Be
Your Own Counsellor* I greatly appreciate. Firstly, to my clients and
students with whom I have had the privilege of working over the
years and from whom I am constantly learning.

More specifically to Gill Cormode and Heather Rocklin of Piatkus
for helpful and constructive editorial advice; and to Carole Blake who
continues her role as a very special agent!

Last, but of course not least, to Cyl who as well as providing
sustaining coffee and almond croissants saw me through the agony
and ecstasy of the new software!

Copyright © 1997 Sheila Dainow
First published in 1996 by
Judy Piatkus (Publishers) Ltd
5 Windmill Street, London W1P 1HF

Reprinted 1997, 1998, 1999

The moral right of the author has been asserted

*A catalogue record for this book is available from
the British Library*

ISBN 0-7499-1586-2

Designed by Sue Ryall

Typeset by Action Typesetting Ltd, Gloucester
Printed and bound in Great Britain by
Biddles Ltd, Guildford and King's Lynn

Contents

Introduction

If you were to compare your life to a journey, starting on the day you were born and due to end on the day you die, how would you describe it? There have probably been times when everything has gone smoothly, when you knew where you were going and were getting there easily. What about the times, though, when the going has been rough? Times, perhaps, when those resources you depended on were depleted, your health weakened or your mind troubled; when other people were behaving badly towards you or unexpectedly leaving you. At such times we feel we have lost our way and can no longer even see the point of the journey.

We all have our own way of facing the problems of living. Sometimes we go it alone, managing as well as we can. Some of us turn to friends or family. On other occasions we might consult professional helpers – doctors, lawyers, social workers, teachers and so on.

Counsellors and therapists are among those who aim to help people to get back on the right track so that life's journey can continue as happily as possible. They use their skill and knowledge to help people understand and take more control of their life. Through a process of regular meeting and talking they work to deepen the client's awareness of the emotional aspects of his or her problems. As clients develop understanding, they can make decisions and take more control over their response to life. The advantage of such helpers is that they have no vested interest in how you decide to run your life. The therapy they offer is an opportunity to evaluate yourself and your life objectively, so that you can make wise and appropriate decisions about the future.

A good counsellor is a creative catalyst for change, aiming to help clients take control of their lives in a productive and satisfying way. Counselling is likely to be less effective if the therapist implies that the changes can only be made by him or her. The danger is that clients' feelings of dependency and powerlessness will be increased by the belief that someone else has to take responsibility for them. If this happens, the counselling process is very likely to end unsatisfactorily – because when the crunch comes it is the client who has to get on with living their life. The counsellor cannot do that for them.

If you have doubts as to whether working through a book could possibly be as effective as being face-to-face with a counsellor, you will be interested to know that several research studies have matched people receiving face-to-face counselling with groups who were given self-help books. In 1992 a review of these studies showed that the people using the books did as well as, or even better than, those actually receiving counselling.

This book explores the idea of becoming your own counsellor and takes you through the various stages of the process. Each chapter mirrors a counselling session, and in working through the various questions and exercises you will be using typical counselling methods to explore yourself and your life with a view to making the changes which you want. The book would also be a useful guide for anyone considering entering a professional counselling relationship as an informed and active partner.

Counsellors and therapists are often criticised for keeping their theories and techniques inaccessible to those who cannot or do not wish to undertake expensive and lengthy training. One of the purposes of this book is to demystify these ideas and make them more available to anyone who is interested in taking charge of their own mental and emotional health.

Using the book

Don't expect to read this book straight through like a novel or textbook. It is intended as a practical manual which can be used in different ways. Each chapter includes an explanation of what a counsellor would be aiming to do at this stage in the process, and includes exercises for you to work on; the last of these is always a reflection exercise so that you can put the process into perspective. If you decide to work systematically through the book on your own you need to allocate a regular time to it. As a rough guide it is wise to think of no less than an hour a week and no more than an hour a day. Make sure that you have a quiet place and will not be interrupted for that time.

Most chapters focus on one particular approach to counselling, so that you are given the opportunity to experience some of the range of techniques. You will find that some methods attract you more than others. If you find that any particular approach does not attract you at all, it is still worth experimenting with using it in the suggested way just to see whether it has something of value to offer you. If it does nothing for you, move on to the next chapter.

You may know yourself well enough to realise that you won't be disciplined enough to do this on your own, or you might in any case prefer to work with other people. If so, you could set up a cooperative partnership with a friend. The best way to organise this is to meet regularly for up to two-hour sessions, splitting the time in half so that you take turns to be 'counsellor' working with your partner 'client'. If you are going to work in this way you would find it useful to read *The Barefoot Psychoanalyst* by John Southgate and Rosemary Randall and *The Upward Trend* by Harvey Jackins. Both these books set out co-counselling techniques and give valuable advice on how to conduct sessions.

Or you might form a group to work together, with each member taking a turn as leader. A useful book to read before starting a group is *In Our Own Hands* by Sheila Ernst and Lucy Goodison.

Whether you are doing the exercises alone or with one other person, read the instructions carefully. You can always refer to the book if you forget them. When you get to places where you are asked to think about something, stop reading and take time to think. You can jot down your thoughts as they occur to you. With some of the longer exercises which ask you to use your imagination you can tape the instructions, and then relax into doing the exercise.

Use your intuition about the pace at which to proceed. You might go through some chapters very quickly, while others might raise many issues that you want time to consider. You may find that unexpected thoughts and memories occur. Sometimes they may be quite disturbing, raising feelings which are unfamiliar or painful. If this happens, talk about them to your partner or fellow group members. If you are on your own, stop working and use one of the meditation or relaxation exercises to help you calm yourself. Then take your time to think about what has happened. If this happens a lot as you work through the book, you might consider employing a counsellor to accompany you on this journey. This would not mean that you had failed. It could be a very positive and constructive decision, and you would enter counselling as a well-informed client.

Self-help is not an easy option because it requires a high level of commitment and discipline; however, there are great rewards to be had. As you get into the habit of giving yourself the time and attention that this work demands, you will feel more in control of yourself and your life.

However you choose to use this book, I wish you a challenging, interesting and educative journey which leads you a destination you desire.

1

What's It All About?

They must change who would be constant in
happiness or wisdom.

Confucius, 551–478 BC

Why go to a counsellor?

*'I was unhappy, but I didn't know why. When I woke up
in the morning I would go through all the reasons why I
should be content: I had a good job, a good home, I had
friends – but it didn't seem to be enough.'*

Jane

*'My problems got on top of me. I couldn't see which way
to turn. People kept giving me advice – what they didn't
seem to understand was that I knew what I probably
should do but just couldn't do it.'*

Stephen

*'I seem to have got into a pattern which keeps repeating
itself. It doesn't seem to make any difference how many
times I try to change, I just find myself doing the same old
thing again.'*

Robin

Jane, Stephen and Robin are talking about why they
decided to use counselling techniques to help them to live

5

more happily. The ways in which they are trying to change things haven't worked very well, so they are looking for a new way to tackle their problems.

You will have your own reasons for wanting to begin. Maybe, like Jane, you have all you need in the material sense but feel somehow that life is empty, that there is something missing. Or perhaps, like Stephen, you are facing many problems and can't see how to get through them. Or you might identify with Robin, who is trying to change old patterns.

The kind of issues that might bring someone to consider counselling vary, but typical examples are:

- conflict in the family
- breakdown of an intimate relationship
- compulsive behaviour
- work problems
- loneliness
- loss of creativity
- concerns regarding sexuality
- feelings of anxiety or depression

It's true to say, though, that you don't have to be distressed, deprived or disturbed to get benefit from counselling. You don't even need to have a problem! You could decide to use the techniques simply to get more out of life or to understand yourself and the people around you better.

The British Association for Counselling defines the overall aim of counselling as providing an opportunity for someone to work towards living in a more satisfying and resourceful way. It may be concerned with:

- developmental issues
- addressing and resolving specific problems
- making decisions
- coping with crisis
- developing personal insight and knowledge

- working through feelings of inner conflict, or
- improving relationships with others.

The counsellor's role is to help in ways which respect the client's values, personal resources and capacity for self-determination.

Counsellors do this by trying to build a special relationship based on mutual trust and respect. The relationship is different from the kind you would normally have with a friend. Your friend, however good a listener, will have his or her own concerns. He or she may have a vested interest in how you deal with problems, and any advice will tend to point you in that direction. Counsellors will, as far as possible, empty their minds of their own concerns and listen attentively to you.

How counselling works

To understand better how counselling works, it's worth thinking about what it's not. It's not the same as going to a doctor or other kind of 'expert' where you are more or less passive and the experts advises, instructs, interprets or directs you. In this kind of relationship the power is rather one-sided, and resides with the expert. In counselling the intention is that the power should be shared. You, as the client, will remain in charge of the 'agenda' – the counsellor is there to help you achieve what you want.

If you are working through this book on your own, think about yourself as the counsellor as well as the client. As your own counsellor you need to give yourself attention, to listen to yourself as carefully as an external counsellor would do. You need to respect rather than punish yourself for not having your life perfectly ordered.

Here is an exercise to help you create the right frame of mind for being a counsellor. It is an imagination exercise, so you need to read it right through before you start.

Alternatively, tape it and play it back to yourself; if you do this, read it slowly with lots of pauses.

EXERCISE

Sit comfortably and spend a couple of minutes relaxing. Focus your mind on your breathing; don't worry if other thoughts intrude. Let them come into your mind, notice what they are, then let them go and return to your awareness of your breathing....

Imagine that you are walking along a winding path through a forest. It is a very pleasant walk – the temperature is warm, but not too hot. You can hear birdsong and the rustling of the leaves on the trees, and you have all the time in the world. As you continue along the path, you notice that it is gently rising and you are climbing upwards.... As you turn a corner you see you are at the top of a hill and there is a seat for you to sit and enjoy the view. You sit down and look at the landscape.... You become aware of another person who has sat down beside you, and as if by magic you know that this person has been accompanying you on the journey even though you were not aware of his or her presence before. This companion has been by your side, not leading in front or pushing from behind, willing to go wherever you wanted. Your companion is willing to continue the journey with you, sometimes shedding light on the path when it is too dark for you to see, sometimes suggesting possible directions, but always willing to go along with your choice. This companion will be by your side, on your side, with only your interest at heart.... You may wish, in your mind's eye, to ask for something from this person. If so, let the dialogue develop.... When you are ready, imagine yourself rising from the seat and retracing your steps, your companion at your side.

You may want to take this a stage further by drawing an image of the companion you imagined, or writing a description. This companion represents your internal counsellor, and you can call on the image as you proceed through the book. You can also work through the exercise with a partner or a group, sharing your images and ideas.

The ground rules of counselling

Although there is a wide range of counselling theories and techniques, most counsellors work to a set of communication 'ground rules' which make the session very different from an ordinary conversation.

Ground rule 1: *listen more; talk less*

Counsellors will use most of their energy listening to what you say and probably won't add any information about themselves to the conversation. It can feel a bit disconcerting if you are not used to being in that situation. He or she will be aiming to create an environment in which you are able to talk about your thoughts and feelings.

When the counsellor does talk he or she is likely to reflect what you have been saying. The aim is to try to empathise with you, to get a view of the world as you see it in order to understand how to be of help. This is why counsellors don't talk very much about themselves.

Here is a series of exercises which will help you practise these counselling skills. All the exercises are described in ways which allow you to do them on your own, or with another person. If you are working in a group, you can divide into pairs and then talk about the whole experience together afterwards. Suggestions for converting the exercises, if you are working on your own, are given.

EXERCISE (a) *Giving Support:*

The most important message that the counsellor needs to get over is: 'I am here to support you.' Sit opposite each other, and in the first instance take it in turns to pretend that you are being the opposite of supportive to your partner. Don't speak, but use your eyes, mouth and body to get over the message. As the recipient, notice what it feels like.

For the second part of this exercise, take it in turns to show that you are wanting to be supportive. Once again, make this a non-verbal communication. You may be surprised at how much you can communicate through your body without words.

If you are working on your own, you can do this exercise in front of a mirror, exaggerating the positions so that you really get a feel for the difference between supporting and non-supporting body language.

EXERCISE (b) *Listening:*

Once again, sit comfortably opposite each other. For five minutes one of you will talk as 'client' and the other will listen as 'counsellor'. When you are talking, talk about something which is on your mind. It doesn't have to be a problem or some deep matter – just something which you have been thinking about and which is interesting enough for you to want to talk about. When you are listening, don't interrupt, ask questions, say things like 'Something just like that happened to me', drift into your own thoughts, judge, criticise or condemn. In fact, don't do anything but listen and communicate your support non-verbally.

Spend five minutes discussing these two exercises.

Now you can communicate in the normal way once again, sharing and exchanging information about your thoughts and feelings.

If you are on your own, sit with a paper and pen. Let your thoughts range for five minutes, and then write down what you can recall of them. If you end up by being surprised at how little attention you are paying to yourself, repeat this exercise until you get into the habit of listening to yourself.

EXERCISE (c) *Reflecting:*

Set up the exercise in the same way, with each of you taking it in turns to practise your skill in reflecting. Start with one of you talking for five minutes about something which is on your mind. The 'counsellor' should pay attention to the speaker's mood and expressions. Pay attention to the quality of the voice – does it sound tense, quiet, nervous, excited and so on. Notice also the other person's hands, body stance and breathing. Give feedback about what you noticed. Then switch round so that you can take the other role. Once again, when the exercise is finished talk about how you felt.

You can practise this on your own with a television or radio. Select a programme on which someone is talking about their personal experience, listen, then switch it off and recall as much as you can. If you are able to tape or video the programme, you have the advantage of being able to check how accurate you were.

These exercises show how counsellors aim to turn their attention fully to the client, listening, supporting and trying to understand the client's experience of the world.

Ground rule 2: *accept the person as he or she is*

The basis of the relationship which a counsellor is aiming to establish is acceptance of you as you are. When someone has a problem or is experiencing difficult feelings, our immediate reaction is to try to make things better. Counsellors will not jump in to smooth away the unhappiness or try to cheer you up. Instead, you will be encouraged to explore and express your feelings fully and to come to terms with things as they are at the present. Questions like 'Can you talk more about what hurts most?' or 'What does it feel like to be so angry?' will push you into analysing your responses. The reason for this is that a distressing feeling does not disappear if we ignore it – it may fade for a while, but it is likely to come up again and again. Counsellors believe that discharging emotions can be a healing process. If a hurt or pain is not released it remains stored up, and a lot of energy can be wasted in keeping it buried. This results in reducing the energy we have available for living day to day.

Perhaps you have experienced the release of having a good cry about something, or the liberation of shouting out your anger. If you have, you will know that, although these expressions of emotion don't solve the problem, you do feel better afterwards.

One of the big advantages of the relationship that counsellors offer is that, as we experience their acceptance of us, we can begin to accept ourselves. Many people are afraid that, if they think well of themselves, they will become self-satisfied and stop developing – but the opposite is more likely to happen. Low self-esteem is at the root of many problems because it erodes our confidence in our ability to manage our lives. Self-acceptance is an important element of self-esteem, and counsellors help us to an assessment of ourselves based on the notion that we are equal to others – not any better, but certainly not any worse.

EXERCISE

This exercise is based on the fairy-tale idea of a fairy godmother. The fairy godmother was someone who unconditionally loved the hero or heroine of the story, always ready to comfort and help in time of trouble. Sit comfortably and take a few calming breaths. Imagine that you have a fairy godmother, building up her image in your mind. Notice what she is wearing, how she looks, the expression on her face. Remember that she loves you whatever you have done.

Now create a scene in your mind's eye where you are with your fairy godmother. Imagine a conversation in which your fairy godmother tells you just how much you are loved and appreciated and reassures you that however much you want to change, she will continue to love and approve of you.

Ground rule 3: *accept responsibility for yourself*

A counsellor will encourage you to recognise and take responsibility for your own feelings, thoughts and behaviour. In our daily lives, we have many different ways of avoiding this. We can blame other people for how we are responding:

- 'If you hadn't reminded me of that, I wouldn't be so unhappy.'
- 'You make me feel guilty.'
- 'I wouldn't lose my temper if you didn't provoke me.'

Each of these responses implies that the other person has got inside you and is controlling your feelings, thoughts and behaviour. What is more likely is that the other person has put you in touch with thoughts and feelings that were already there. It would be truer to say:

- 'I was able to hide how unhappy I was until you uncovered it.'
- 'When I think about you, I feel guilty.'
- 'I lose control over my anger when I perceive you as provoking me.'

Another way we can avoid taking responsibility is by criticising other people for feelings which actually belong to us. Remarks like:

- 'You're too competitive.'
- 'You want too much attention.'
- 'I wish you weren't so picky.'

could be translated into:

- 'I feel competitive towards you.'
- 'I'm jealous because I want some of the attention you have.'
- 'I feel nervous when you challenge me on details.'

A counsellor will prompt you to explore your feelings about yourself rather than your feelings about the other person. In this way he or she will help you own what you are actually feeling rather than project those feelings on to someone else.

Another type of projection takes place when feelings from the past get transferred on to something that is happening in the present. For example, suppose you feel very angry at someone who is ignoring you. It is possible that the intensity of your anger is fuelled by times in the past when you felt ignored – perhaps by important figures from your childhood like your parents or siblings. While this doesn't invalidate your anger at the present person who may be behaving badly, it is useful to be clear about where your anger is coming from. Otherwise, you may respond with behaviour which is out of all proportion to the importance of the present event. We all tend to displace feelings this way; in fact it is a very good check to ask yourself, 'Does this person remind me of anybody?' whenever you feel intensely towards someone. This will prevent you from leaping in to attack someone who is irritating you.

You will often find that a counsellor will focus on the language you are using and suggest that you change certain words or phrases to reflect the responsibility you bear for your responses. You might say, for instance, 'Jennifer is insensitive and thoughtless. I hate her. She never takes any notice of what I say.' The counsellor might suggest you change this to, 'I'm feeling irritated with Jennifer. She didn't acknowledge what I said at the meeting.' Through discussion with the counsellor, you might also realise that your feeling is a familiar one and that your anger is directed at other people in your life who never seemed to take you seriously.

Sometimes these can seem very petty points – after all, we know what we mean! But in practice they are useful devices to stop us avoiding feelings which we could benefit from exploring and expressing.

EXERCISE *Owning Your Feelings:*

Once again, this can be done with a partner or by yourself, recording your responses. The point is to make a series of statements about how you are feeling at the present time. Start each statement 'I am feeling ... and I own this feeling'. Examples:

- 'I'm feeling tired and I own this feeling.'
- 'I feel left out and I own this feeling.'
- 'I feel self-conscious talking in this way and I own the feeling.'

You might find that the things you say sound trivial or

---

obvious, like 'I'm feeling hot' or 'My left foot itches',
but include them all the same. The point of the exercise is to give you practice in expressing just what you
are feeling at the moment. As a result you may begin to
notice how your feelings, although they may be triggered by some external force, actually come from
within yourself.

Ground rule 4: *listen to the body language*

We live in a society which tends to value minds above
bodies. From an early age we are taught how to behave
reasonably and keep ourselves under control. Our bodies
are programmed to prepare us for fight or flight whenever
we perceive a threat, but most of the time we can't fight in
the physical sense or rush screaming from the room when
our safety is jeopardised. We subdue our natural response
and face the situation. It isn't that this is a bad thing – after
all, we couldn't really have a society in which everyone
reacted as if every threat was a matter of life and death. The
problem is that we can take things to the other extreme and
hide our natural emotional responses altogether. Our mind
takes over, and signals from our body are ignored.

In counselling, you will be encouraged to pay attention
and respect to the messages you get from your body. For
instance, breathing is a very important indicator of the level
of stress we are experiencing. We tend to breathe very shal-
lowly as an unconscious way of cutting off from what we are
feeling. Full breathing is a useful way of relaxing our
muscles and getting in touch with ourselves, so that feelings
which have been suppressed come more easily to the fore. If
the counsellor notices that, as you are speaking, your body
is becoming tense and your breathing shallow, he or she
may point this out and suggest you breathe more deeply
and slowly.

Here are some exercises to try. They will help you raise your awareness of your body and will be a useful preparation for dealing with any stressful situation.

EXERCISE *Breathing Awareness:*

This exercise can be done in the same way as the earlier imagination exercise. Have someone read it out, or record it and then play it back to yourself.

Lie on the floor or sit in a chair which gives you good support, preferably with your shoes off and your clothing loosened. Become aware of your breathing.... Breathe in through your nose and out through your mouth.... As you breathe out each time, imagine that you are breathing out the tension in your body ... let your body become heavier with each breath as you let your muscles relax.... Imagine that you are sinking into the floor or chair with each out-breath.... Keep your awareness on your breathing, noticing how it feels when the air is drawn into your nose, throat and lungs and how it feels when you breathe it out through your mouth.... Don't worry if other thoughts intrude – let them come, then let them drift out of your mind and return to your awareness of your breathing.... Now with each out-breath make a sighing noise.... Place one hand on your abdomen just below your navel. When you breathe in, imagine that you are breathing into your hand ... let it rise on the in-breath and fall again on the out-breath.... Breathe out slowly with a sigh, letting all the breath out of your lungs each time.... Breathe like this for a while and then, when you are ready to finish, slowly get up and stretch.

You can let this exercise develop into a relaxation by continuing as follows. Now focus your awareness on your feet and curl up your toes, making the muscles in your feet tense. As you breathe in, exaggerate the

---

tension, and when you breathe out, relax your feet and imagine you are breathing out all the tension in your feet. Repeat a few times.

Now focus on your legs. Tighten the muscles in your calves, knees, thighs.... As you breathe in, tighten right up. Then as you breathe out, let the tension go ... feeling your legs getting heavier with each repetition....

Repeat this pattern up the body, focusing in turn on your pelvis, abdomen, chest, shoulders, arms, neck, head and face. Finish with relaxing the whole body as at the beginning.

EXERCISE *Speaking without Words:*

Sit facing a partner or a mirror; take three minutes to have a conversation or express a feeling without words. Use your body to the full – gestures, expressions and so on.

This is marvellous practice in using your body as a communicator, thus deepening the range of communication tools you have available. You might be surprised at the range of communication you can achieve without using words at all.

These ground rules are at the basis of the kind of counselling which is often called 'client-centred'. The American psychologist Carl Rogers was a great influence on the development of modern counselling methods. He felt that, if counsellors were able to create the kind of relationship in which the client felt valued and free to explore his or her thoughts and feelings, therapeutic success was likely to follow. He wrote about the different types of counselling in which he was engaged, which ranged from brief contacts with clients who came for practical advice to long-term and intensive psychotherapy, 'I have come to the conclusion that one learning which applies to all of these experiences is that it is the quality of the personal relationship which matters most.'

There are one or two other ground rules to which most counsellors adhere. These are of a slightly different nature, in that they are about the environment within which the counselling takes place.

Ground rule 5: *no violence*

Counsellors will encourage you to express your anger safely by talking about it, role playing what you want to say or even hitting a cushion. While working through this book with other people you may want to use these strategies. Of course, actual violence towards another person would never be condoned by a counsellor.

Ground rule 6: *no drugs/alcohol*

There are all sorts of substances we can use to help us control ourselves. Cigarettes, alcohol, drugs, coffee and tea are examples. Most counsellors insist that you do not drink alcohol or take drugs before or during sessions. Many will also have rules about smoking and drinking coffee and tea.

You might decide against having strict rules about things like coffee or tea, but it is worth noticing when you reach for a cigarette or drink because this will make you more aware of what is upsetting you and how you may be trying to mask the feelings. This awareness will help you understand how you can deal with the matter in a different way from covering it up.

Ground rule 7: *confidentiality*

All counselling should take place under a contract of confidentiality. You need to feel free to explore your thoughts and feelings in the knowledge that the counsellor will not gossip about you. People often expose themselves more intimately to a counsellor than to anyone else in their lives, and it is important that this trust is not betrayed. If you are using this book with other people, you need to make an agreement not to discuss with anyone else what you learn about each other as a result of the work you do.

Reflection

This chapter has set the scene for counselling by explaining what the counsellor would be aiming to do and by giving you an opportunity to practise some of the skills.

Before you start on Chapter 2, take time to reflect on that scene. The aim of counselling is to provide an opportunity for you to consider yourself and your life without making blaming judgements on yourself or on anyone else. Taking stock of the past and making decisions about the future is the purpose of this particular journey. When you feel ready for the next step, move on.

2

Beginning to Change

The first step is the hardest.

Traditional proverb

The natural resistance that we seem to have to change sometimes surprises or angers others, particularly those who are trying to change for the better. We need to understand this resistance, because the whole point of counselling is to make changes. You might want to make dramatic changes – for instance to change your whole lifestyle, end a relationship or move into a new career. On the other hand, the changes you want could be more subtle – perhaps changing your perception of a situation or becoming more comfortable with your emotional responses. Whether the changes are big or small, understanding how you might unconsciously hinder them will help you ensure that resistance is no impediment to your success.

Why are human beings so resistant to change? We are, after all, probably the most adaptable of living creatures. One day is never exactly the same as another. People survive in many different social and physical environments, going through many changes in the course of their lives. Perhaps it is because our environment is so changeable that we are so concerned with making it predictable. It would be hard to survive even for a day if we had no way of knowing what was going to happen next. So we try to impose regularity on events which never can be absolutely regular.

As a society, for instance, we have created a system of laws to help us understand and place some order on our physical world. Every society creates a system of rules which limits people's behaviour towards each other in some way. Different societies have created very diverse systems. Just think how different European, Oriental and African societies are from each other. Each system is affected by its own development and history; our own awareness is different now from how it was one or two hundred years ago. Our system of law is changing all the time to reflect the changes we experience.

Just as we try to impose order on our physical and social world, we attempt to do the same for our internal, emotional world. When we are born, we don't have enough knowledge about the world to keep ourselves safe. We have to depend on the adults around us to do that. It's a pity we aren't born with a guidebook which tells us all we need to know. Think how much easier infancy would be if, by some magic, you could read a book which told you, for instance, 'You aren't going to feel comfortable all the time. The people looking after you are not very good at knowing what you want, and you don't know their language well enough to tell them. But they are trying; so you can afford to relax. If they don't do what you want immediately, don't assume that you have been abandoned or are unloved. They are doing their best and will work out what you need and give it to you as soon as they can.'

However, as babies we don't know this; all we know is what we are feeling and experiencing in the present moment. If we are hungry, we don't know that we are ever going to be fed; if we are cold, we don't know how to get warm – and so on. As far as we know, we have to survive somehow in this confusing and dangerous place.

Right from our very first moments, we instinctively try to understand life so that we can make it as predictable as possible. This process can be described as making a mental map to help us negotiate the unknown and frightening territory in which we find ourselves. Learning how this map that we created as children is still influencing us in our adult lives is often a substantial element in counselling, and will be looked at in more detail in the following chapters.

A safe space

There are some practical matters to be settled before you start on the work you want to do. Because counselling is so much about change it is important that you create a safe environment in which to work. Counsellors give a great deal of consideration to this, realising that the atmosphere in which the counselling takes place is extremely influential. Most counselling, for instance, takes place within regular sessions for which appointments have to be made.

One of the problems of undertaking self-help counselling, of course, is that you don't have the structure created for you. If you know someone is expecting you at a particular place at a particular time you are likely to be there. If they expect to be paid, whether you attend or not, you are very, very likely to be there! It is more difficult to motivate ourselves with no one else taking the responsibility.

Take the opportunity now to give thought to the place and time of your counselling sessions.

The place

Most counsellors take great care that their offices provide an environment which will minimise stress. You need to choose a room in which you can be quiet and uninterrupted for the times you select.

The room doesn't have to be luxurious but it should be one in which you feel comfortable. Make sure the temperature is not too warm or too cold, and that there is a comfortable chair. It will be useful to have a table available.

If you intend to work through this book with another person, discuss where you will meet. You could take it in turns to provide the room. If you are working as a group, hiring a room might be the only way you can get enough space. You need a room where you can all sit round in a circle on comfortable chairs.

The time

When you have decided upon the place, you need to think about the time. Choose a regular time and keep to it. Most counselling sessions last for a minimum of fifty minutes and a maximum of ninety minutes, and take place at regular weekly or fortnightly intervals. If you are working on your own, an hour is probably the most reasonable time to set aside. If you are working with a partner, two and a quarter hours enables you to work for an hour and have time for the changeover; if you are working as a group, two to three hours would be a good timespan. Take care that whatever arrangement you decide upon is a reasonable one for you. Don't set yourself up to fail by making an arrangement that will just be too much for you to maintain. Deciding to give yourself two hours every day may sound good, but if you know you won't be able to keep it up choose something more reasonable.

When you have decided on the details of when and where, write them down in your diary.

A contract for change

Having dealt with the practical arrangements for your counselling, you need to give consideration to the reasons for the whole undertaking. What is it you want to achieve?

When working with a new client, a counsellor will spend time at the beginning clarifying the client's expectations. These may range from the very practical, such as 'I want to succeed in the job interview I'm going to', to more emotional issues such as 'My partner left me years ago but I just can't get over the rage I feel.' Sometimes people have unrealistic hopes that the counsellor will be able to produce some magic which will solve all their problems. At the other end of the scale some clients come with a sense of hopelessness, certain that no one can possibly help them.

Although a counsellor often cannot produce solutions to problems, he or she can help to identify the changes which might be needed in order for the situation to improve. If the client accepts that these changes would be beneficial, the two of them can then work together to bring them about.

Most counsellors will want to make a contract with the client early in the process, and this is usually linked to the desired outcome. In this way both parties will be clear about the direction of the work. A contract has other advantages, too: it enables an assessment of progress to be made, and it is a benchmark for knowing when the work is completed. Otherwise – if neither the practitioner nor the client is clear about the finishing point – there is a danger that counselling may drag on for months or even years.

So your first task when you begin self-counselling is to make a contract. We have already considered the practical details of time and place. Now it is time to think about the purpose.

The purpose

Here is one structure for making a contract which you can use whether working alone, or with a partner or group.

EXERCISE

This is your first counselling session. So you need to gather together writing or taping materials and make sure you have set aside the necessary uninterrupted time in which to work.

First Stage: write down the changes you want to make.

Don't worry about what words to use. Just write down whatever comes to mind. This is not an essay and you don't have to show it to anyone or get it marked or judged for literary merit. You may find it easier to speak your thoughts into a recorder first – then write them down. Obviously, if you are working with other people, you can take it in turns to tell each other your wishes.

When you have finished, read it over and notice the kind of language you have used. Where possible, a contract should be phrased positively. Do you, for instance, want to *stop* smoking, *never* lose your temper, *quit* drinking, *not* be so unassertive? Change these statements if you can into positive outcomes like 'I will become a non-smoker'; 'I will control my temper'; 'I will stand up for my rights'. The problem is that you cannot see yourself not doing something. Try now to imagine yourself not sitting down. You will find that in order to create a picture of yourself *not* sitting down, you first have to think about yourself sitting down! If you can picture yourself in a positive light, you will feel more like doing the work required to achieve success.

Another reason is that everything we do fulfils some need for us, and sometimes the power of the need overrides our better judgement. For instance, Andrew is very shy; he wants to enjoy social occasions but every time he is with other people he becomes very quiet and withdrawn. He feels anxious and uncomfortable. It is easy to understand why he wants to change, but less easy to be clear about why it is so difficult. As Andrew thought more about why he behaves the way he does in a crowd, he realised that he was very afraid of rejection. His 'shyness' protects him from that fear. For as long as he keeps distant from people, they can't reject him.

Andrew had on his list of wants 'I don't want to be shy.' He changed it to 'I want to enjoy being with people.'

- If necessary, rewrite your wants in positive language.

EXERCISE: *Second Stage*

This stage consists of asking yourself a series of questions about the changes you have identified.

---

1. Can this change be measured?　We sometimes set ourselves up to fail because we decide on something which is too vague. For instance, 'I want to be more assertive'; 'I mean to be happier'; 'I am going to improve my health.' There is nothing wrong with any of these wishes; the problem is that, as they are stated at the moment, they are not specific enough and can't be measured. How much is 'more'? What does 'happier' really mean? When is 'improvement' enough? 'I want to be able to put my point of view in a discussion and, if someone disagrees with me, to argue my case without giving in or losing my temper' is an example of a change stated in more specific terms.

2. Is this change possible for you?　Another trap is to set a goal which depends on other people changing. It is not possible to guarantee a change in other people. The only person over whom you have that kind of control is yourself; so, to ensure the possibility of your success with this contract, it must be about something which you yourself have the resources to achieve.

3. Do you have the necessary resources?　It's also a bad idea to decide on a goal which demands resources you do not have at the moment. 'I want to travel the world' is a wish that requires money and time. If you have neither, it would be more sensible to think about how you can get the resources and make a contract accordingly – or modify the wish to something for which you do have the means.

4. Do you know anyone who has achieved what you want? It will help to have a model of the result for which you are hoping. We developed many of our present behaviour patterns by observing the models we had early on in life – parents, teachers, siblings and so on. In fact, sometimes the greatest problem is that behaviour which was very appropriate to that time in our life has become a habit – it may not be so appropriate at the present time. As adults we are in a better position to choose our models, so that we can see what we are aiming for.

5. What will actually be different when you have achieved your desired change? Define in detail what you and others will be able to see and hear you doing differently. If the change you want concerns how you relate to other people, specify the people involved by name. You might be aiming, for instance, to be a more confident public speaker. In this case you might come up with 'I would be breathing easily, smiling, taking my time and enjoying the experience. I would have prepared well in advance and have rehearsed so that I am familiar with what I want to say. If someone asks a question, I will thank them and take my time in answering. If I don't know the answer, I will say so and offer to check later.'

6. Are the changes you are contemplating safe for you? Check that the changes you want are physically safe and socially appropriate. One way of meeting new people would be to talk to strangers in the street, but it could be risky. You can become more assertive with your employer, but don't put your job at risk unless you are prepared for the consequences. Clarify for yourself what you are and are not ready to risk to make the changes you want.

7. How much is the change really for you? Check that this change is for your own development rather than to get someone else's approval or to rebel against someone. Whether these 'someones' are from the past or the present, if your contract is being made more for their benefit than for yours you are likely to end up still feeling dissatisfied and not in control of your life.

8. What might the cost be of achieving the changes? Every change involves gains and losses. Think carefully about the possible costs and check that you still want to make the change.

EXERCISE: *Third Stage*

Return to your original statement, which you may want to modify in the light of your answers. Rewrite the statement in simple, direct language. One way of doing this is to imagine that you want to explain it to an intelligent eight-year-old. This is a wonderful way of guarding against getting too wordy and complicated.

Cordelia started by saying, 'I want my husband to make me happier. I don't want to continue as we are.' She then reframed her contract into: 'I want to understand why I feel unhappy in my marriage and then decide what to do for the future.' This is a contract which will help her take responsibility for what is happening in her marriage and clarify the actual changes she is hoping for.

Frances started with 'I'm treated like a doormat at work. I want to get more respect. I'd like to tell my boss exactly what I think about her.' Her reframed contract was 'I want to tell my employer how I feel when I am treated unfairly.' This seemed a more practical and less risky way of improving things at work.

For the people concerned, each of these contracts is a

step along the way towards much larger changes. Trying to understand the possible roots of unhappiness is an important step before making decisions; telling someone how you feel about their behaviour will contribute considerably towards general assertiveness.

Devising a satisfactory contract is an important part of the counselling process. It can be compared to having a compass on a journey in unknown territory. If you get lost, the compass will always point you in the right direction. For a while, you might want to take a side track that looks very interesting; the compass will always help you back on to the main path if you have taken a wrong turn.

Just as the compass itself cannot make the journey for you, your contract won't effect the changes you want. But just as the compass will always tell you which way you should be facing, the contract will help you focus your energy on the task at hand.

Reflection

This is the end of your first counselling session. You have made a contract to help you clarify the direction in which you want to go. Take time to reflect on what you think and feel about the work you have done. Congratulate yourself for reaching this point. Even if you have a long way to go, the first step in any journey is often the most difficult – and you have taken it. Give yourself a reward for the time and trouble you have taken. It doesn't have to be expensive – just something which is significant to you to mark your effort in a positive way. Settling down to watch a good play on TV; going for a walk; buying yourself flowers; asking for a hug from your nearest and dearest – all these are good examples. You will know just what will give you pleasure, and this is a good time for you to indulge yourself.

3

Telling the Story

...I will a round unvarnish'd tale deliver....

William Shakespeare, Othello

In Chapter 2 you thought about your reasons for taking on counselling and made a contract. Returning to our analogy of a journey, this is like deciding why you want to travel and where you want to go. However, in order actually to start the journey you have to know where you are. This brings us to the next counselling task, which is to make an assessment of your present situation.

Although this sounds simple enough, it is perhaps the most difficult part to do on your own. One of the most therapeutic elements of going to another person for counselling is the fact that you will have their undivided attention for the time of the session. The quality of this attention helps you unfold the story of your situation. If the counsellor is not only attentive but also non-judgemental, you can explore your thoughts and feelings without the usual worries about what people will think of you. The first part of this chapter offers a way to connect with yourself without making the kind of judgements which might get in the way of your objectivity.

Frequently, our harshest judge and critic is ourself. If this is true for you, refer to the exercise in Chapter 1 when you created the image of a companion who would represent your internal counsellor (see p. 9) If this was a real person, he or she would help you to understand what was happening without judging you as good or bad, silly or sensible, clever or stupid. Those judgements are not helpful because they are usually being made against some mental measure which is not reliable. The reason it is not reliable is that we tend to develop your own value systems, our idea of what's right and what's wrong, very early in our life. So the measure may be archaic, because what might have been appropriate then may not be so appropriate now.

Labels that stick

Even though your present behaviour might not be solving the problem, judging it without understanding what lies behind it is unproductive. The judgement does not in itself help to effect a change.

EXERCISE *Part 1:*

This exercise is designed to heighten your awareness of the way you might be judging yourself which can be harmful to your development.

Start by writing down a list of all the things for which you criticise yourself. Include small things as well as the more important matters; don't be put off by thinking that some things are too trivial to count.

As you look over the list, do you find yourself thinking things like 'That's just how I am'; 'I've always been like that'; 'I can't help it.' If you do, then you have a clue that you are actually hanging on to labels which prevent your changing and developing your potential. Many of these labels can be traced to something you learned in the past, and each time you use one of these statements it is as if you are really saying, '… and I intend to stay the same.'

Here is a typical list which might match your own:

- I'm shy
- I'm too fat
- I'm clumsy
- I'm poor at mathematics
- I'm not musical
- I'm no good at sports
- I'm accident-prone
- I'm too serious
- I'm obstinate

- I'm too short-tempered
- I'm undisciplined
- I'm careless
- I'm irresponsible
- I'm a poor cook
- I'm a bad listener
- I'm selfish
- I'm lazy
- I'm unsociable

How did you first get these labels? There are two possibilities. The first is that someone else gave it to you, probably when you were a child and had no way of assessing how accurate it was. Take Catherine as an example. She is eight and loves painting. She has a great deal of fun in the art class at school, experimenting with colours and splashing the paint around. Her teacher tells her that she will never be good at art. Catherine believes the teacher and begins to try to make her paintings fit in with what the others are doing. She gets less and less enjoyment out of the sessions and as soon as possible gives up art. She tells herself 'I'm no good at art', and will probably carry around this label for the rest of her life.

Do you remember anyone saying to you something like, 'You take after your Auntie Kate – she was no good at English either', or 'She's going to be shy, just like me.'

John, who was always criticising himself for being lazy, remembers how his parents were worried that he might not fulfil their wish for him to be a successful academic. Whenever he seemed to be relaxing, they would berate him for being lazy. In fact he worked very hard, and it was their fear that he would stop that motivated their criticism. But what John caught was the 'lazy' label, and it has turned out to be a problem. He never feels he is working hard enough;

when he takes a rest he feels guilty and worried that he is somehow on the slippery slope to 'laziness'.

Another way that you might have become attached to a particular label is because it enables you to avoid risky, unpleasant or tedious activities. Debbie is at the stage in life when her children are grown up and she could turn her dream to go to university into reality. But each time she talks about this she experiences her fear of failure and worry about competing with young people who might be intellectually superior. So although she regularly sends away for prospectuses, she thinks to herself, 'I couldn't do it; I'm too old now; I'm not clever enough.' It is true that she would need to work hard and that some of it might prove tedious or difficult. It is true that she would have to get accustomed to an unfamiliar environment and that most of the students would be younger than her. It is true that the situation would present challenges and risks. However, it is *not* true that she is too old or not clever enough. Debbie is using her labels to avoid facing the risks inherent in something she really wants.

EXERCISE *Part 2:*

Think carefully about the labels you have identified. Are any of them just convenient ways of not having to face the time and trouble it would take to change? Decide either to continue being this way, or to begin the work necessary for change. Notice any labels which you were given but which were never true, or are now out of date. You should now be able to rewrite each item, prefacing each with one of the following:

- I choose to....
- Until today I was....
- I used to label myself as....

What is happening in your life?

As you begin to tell the story of what is happening in your life, watch out for any ways in which you are making judgements on yourself. There will be time later to assess how effectively you are managing, but that is not the purpose of this particular exercise.

EXERCISE

If you are working by yourself, get comfortably settled with a tape recorder or paper and a pen. Begin to tell your story. What is happening to you at the moment? What has led you to try counselling? Use the suggested structure if you feel it would help, but don't follow it slavishly – it's meant to be a guide, not a rigid framework. Let yourself relax into telling your story your way.

   If you are working with a partner or a group, give each other time to talk. The next section of this chapter tells you some of the things to listen for and possible questions. You may wish to read it before you begin and use some of the ideas as you talk to each other. The following framework of questions will help you begin.

What is actually happening to you now?

Keep the answer to this question a specific description of what *is* happening, not what you *think* might be happening. For instance:

- I am getting very bad headaches.
- I lose my temper and say things I regret later.
- I seem to be trapped in an unhappy relationship.

What is not happening?

This question is useful because the problem often revolves more around what is not happening than around what is actually taking place.

- I know I should look for work, but I haven't been doing it.
- I've made an action plan, but I'm not keeping to it.
- I'm not standing up for myself.

What are other people doing or not doing?

This question helps you to separate yourself from the other people involved. You need to take responsibility for what you are doing – not for what others are doing. By the same token, you may need to confront others with their responsibilities.

- She ignores me when I speak to her.
- He takes my things without asking.
- The boss make jokes at my expense.

What are you thinking?

Distinguishing between thought, feeling and action is an important factor in deciding what and how to change. When our senses perceive something, we react by thinking; those thoughts create our physical and emotional response. This leads to whatever action we take. While we are experiencing this it all seem to happen at once, but the process can be separated. Changing your perceptions and how you think about a situation will inevitably change how you feel and then what you do in response.

- I'm sure she doesn't love me.
- I don't think I'm clever enough to pass the exams.
- I'm worried that I might have cancer.

What are you feeling?

Your feelings are a product of the way you are thinking. Imagine seven drivers lined up behind each other in a traffic jam.

- Driver 1 thinks, 'This always happens to me.'
- Driver 2 thinks, 'It's all the fault of the government – they should have a proper traffic policy.'
- Driver 3 thinks, 'I'm going to be late – people will be very cross.'
- Driver 4 thinks, 'This is hopeless – I'm stuck here for ever.'
- Driver 5 thinks, 'I hope my date waits for me.'
- Driver 6 thinks, 'I wish the car behind wasn't so close.'
- Driver 7 thinks, 'Oh good, a chance to relax.'

Each of these drivers is in the same situation – stuck in a traffic jam – but each of them has a different experience.

- Driver 1 feels resignation and sadness.
- Driver 2 feels blaming and resentful.
- Driver 3 feels fear.
- Driver 4 feels hopeless.
- Driver 5 feels anxious.
- Driver 6 feels threatened.
- Driver 7 feels composed and unruffled.

Whatever they are thinking and feeling will not change the situation. This is why it is important that we take responsibility for our thoughts and feelings rather than assume they are caused by someone or something outside of us. It may seem as though someone else is making you feel what you feel, but this is not really so. Although you can, and should, hold others accountable for their behaviour towards you, you cannot blame them for how you are feeling:

- I feel full of rage.
- Since he left, I've been feeling sad.
- I feel ashamed of myself.
- I'm very anxious, but I don't really know why.

What are you doing?

You will be reacting in some way to the thoughts and feelings you have described, and it may well be that this behaviour is contributing to the problem. When you answer this question, try to analyse your actual behaviour – rather than say what you think you ought to be doing.

- I shout at my partner.
- I drink more than I should.
- I withdraw from contact with people.
- I have a panic attack.

What would you prefer to be happening?

This question will help you clarify the changes you want.

- I know I'd feel better if I changed my priorities.
- I want to be making decisions about the future.
- I want to lose weight.

What would you be doing if you were succeeding?

Visualising the effects of the changes you desire is an important step to understanding what you will actually need to do.

- When I wake up, I would be thinking positively about the day.

- I would be controlling my eating – replacing chocolates and cakes with fruit and vegetables.

What are you willing to do to start?

Every journey, no matter how long, starts with one step. Deciding on your first step will make your journey seem practical and possible.

- When I feel a panic attack coming on, I'd be willing to stop whatever it is that I'm doing and do my breathing exercises.
- I could make a list of the foods I know are bad for me.
- I am willing to talk about my feelings.

How is that different from what you are actually doing?

This is another question to encourage you to think in a practical way about what you want.

- I'm trying to ignore the problem.
- I let myself be taken over by my anger.
- At the moment I am not confident enough to send off the application forms I have filled out.

What is the worst that could happen if you start to change?

We often prevent ourselves from making changes by fearing what might happen. Facing those fears in your thoughts will help you assess them realistically.

- She might get angry and leave me.
- They will laugh at me and I'll feel stupid.
- Things could stay the same.

How might you sabotage yourself?

You probably know exactly how you might get in the way of
your progress by thinking, feeling or acting in familiar but
unhelpful ways.

- By blaming other people for what I was doing.
- By sinking into self-pity.
- By believing others always know better than I do.

These are all useful questions which will help you explore,
define and clarify your situation in a practical way. It would
be a good idea to stop reading now and finish telling your
story. It is quite possible that your work so far has started
off many thoughts and feelings which you need time to
explore. You may choose to take a break altogether and
return to the work later.

Shaping our personality

If you were telling your story to a counsellor, he or she
would be listening to more than the words. The counsellor
would be listening for ways in which you reveal your experience of the world.

The way we choose to present ourselves gives important
clues to the way we see our inner world. How much of our
personality is due to our response to our infant and childhood experiences and how much is determined by the genes
we inherit before our birth is not known. The balance of the
influence of nature versus nurture has often been disputed.
Many experts believe that the environment we grow up in is
the decisive factor, others that heredity is the crucial factor.

Whatever it is that shapes human nature, each one of us
consciously has to create an understanding of the life in
which we find ourselves. This process has been likened to
making a map or a model which we can use as an aid to

making decisions about what we should do to survive. This representation determines to a large degree how we perceive the choices available to us as we go through life.

No two people seem to have exactly the same map. People born into the same family often have different perceptions of what happens to them. The next exercises aims to demonstrate this point.

EXERCISE

Stand by an open window and look at the view. If you don't have a window handy, imagine that you are looking at a beautiful landscape through an open window. Now close (or imagine that you close) the window and notice the differences. They might be great – for instance the window might be dirty, or the glass distorted. Or the change might be very subtle, perhaps just a small mark on the glass or some part of the view cut off by the frame.

Collect some different types of spectacles and sunglasses and experiment with each of them, noticing how they change the view you have.

Just as our sight is affected by different filters, our perceptions are affected by mental filters like:

- individual genetic inheritance which predisposes us in certain ways
- the time and place of our birth and the family into which we were born
- our particular personality – the collection of likes, dislikes, moral values, habits and so on which go to make up our individual response

For instance, two brothers growing up in the same family might develop very different perceptions of their world. One might say, 'My parents were very caring but I knew that they really preferred my brother. They tried to be fair, but they definitely liked him better.' The other might say, 'I was very unhappy as a child. My parents didn't love me as much as they loved my brother and they never hid the fact.' The parents' point of view is that they were trying their hardest not to show either child any favoured treatment! Each of the brothers has created his own model of the world they shared.

The influential nature of these models can be seen in the way that people manage crisis points in their life. Some have little difficulty, experiencing them as times of challenge, excitement and creativity; while others, faced with the same situations, experience fear, anxiety and pain. One way of explaining such different responses to similar situations is that everyone is making choices out of their own particular model. It is not so much that people are making the wrong choices; rather their model does not offer them enough options.

Two American therapists, John Grinder and Richard Bandler, noticed how people seemed to reveal their model of perception through the way they used language. One common aim of counsellors, whatever their approach, is to help the client experience life as richer and better so as to function more successfully in the world. Being able to appreciate the nature of the model the client is operating from will make it easier to understand where change would be appropriate.

In their book *The Structure of Magic*, Bandler and Grinder developed what they called their Meta-model for raising awareness of the clues about our inner world which we give in the way we talk. Here are some of the common language patterns which Bandler and Grinder felt could get in the way of people understanding each other.

What's missing?

Sometimes the way in which we talk makes it difficult for others to understand our experience fully. Each person's model of the world remains hidden, but it is tempting to believe that everyone sees things in the same way. Deletion refers to what is left out of a sentence. Although we don't really know what the person means, we fill in the blanks with our own assumptions. Someone says, for instance, 'I'm confused'; we don't know about what or whom, but we might assume we do and continue the conversation on that basis. In order to understand as much as possible about the way a person is experiencing their world, you can ask questions which will clarify things. For example:

• I'm angry	About what? About whom?
• I'm ready	What are you ready to do?
• I'm feeling better	Better about what?
• I don't know what to do	Do about what?
• She is the best	Compared to whom?
• Please help me	What kind of help do you want?

Vague pronouns

Pronouns are the little words which we use to represent the subject to which we are referring. Because they are not specific, confusion and misinterpretation can easily occur. Here are some examples:

• *It's* unfair	What's unfair
• *They* say it can't be done	Who says it can't be done?
• *That's* wrong	What's wrong?
• *This* must stop	What must stop?
• *It's* all her fault	How is it her fault? What did she do?

Vague verbs

Some verbs, too, can be very unspecific, leaving you with a lot to work out for yourself. For instance, someone might say, 'You irritate me!' You realise they are not happy with you, but what are you actually doing which is irritating? Is the person irritated all the time or just some of the time? Is the behaviour which causes the problem something you are willing to change? Here are some more examples with the questions you can ask to get clearer:

• She *hurts* me all the time	In what way does she hurt you?
• I *like* him	What do you like about him?
• I want to keep *moving*	How do you want to keep moving? Where to?
• I don't like being *pushed*	How are you being pushed? What are you being pushed towards?

Vague nouns

Nouns are words to represent people, places or things. Vague nouns are not so specific, but are still used as if they were concrete things or events. It's easy to distinguish them from the others. Visualise a box and imagine putting an apple, an orange, a paper clip and an envelope in it. These are all nouns. Now imagine placing some guilt, a problem, a relationship in the box. These are also nouns, but how can you see them? *The problem, our relationship, our guilt, your success* are examples of vague nouns or nominalisations. Someone who talks about 'our guilt', for example, will know what they mean. But other people may have different models of guilt and interpret the message wrongly. Here are examples of nominalisations and questions that would challenge them:

• I'm unhappy with our *relationship*	What is it you are unhappy with?
• I'm full of *guilt*	Guilt about what or whom?

- The *problem* is too big to solve

  What does the problem consist of? What have you already tried?

- It's a *misunderstanding*

  What is it that is being misunderstood?

Getting the full message

This attention to language is a very practical way of clarifying communication so that the full story comes over. Bandler and Grinder also had ideas about challenging the limits of a person's model, which you might also like to use. The following patterns are those which could be restricting your experience in an artificial way.

Absolutes

These are generalisations embodied in words such as *always, never, everyone, all, none, no one.* When someone says, 'No one ever listens to me!' it is unlikely that this is the truth. What is probably happening is that someone who is important in their life is not taking enough notice of them. Once that is established, it would be possible to begin solving the problem. Here are some examples, together with the questions which will help encourage exploration:

- *No one ever* listens to me

  Can you think of any occasion when someone did listen to you?

- She *always* argues with me

  Can you think of any time when she agreed with you?

Unnecessary limits

These are the words which imply that you have no choice – words like *can't, must, it's impossible.* Words like *should, must, ought* have to carry the weight of a moral imperative and imply that you are somehow a bad person if you don't obey. Challenging these absolutes is a way of encouraging someone to explore options before they make up their mind.

- I *can't* speak about it   What stops you speaking?
- It's *impossible*   What is it that's impossible?
- I *have* to do what he says   What would happen if you didn't obey him?
- You *ought* to listen   What would happen if I didn't?

Generalisations

Whenever you say something like 'Modern music is rubbish' or 'Politicians are power-hungry' or 'It isn't worth being angry' you are displaying some part of your view of the world and closing off any other possibility. These statements, too, are worth challenging:

- Your work is not satisfactory   What, specifically, is not satisfactory about my work?
- Men just don't understand women   What has happened to lead you to believe that?

These suggestions show how it is possible to express your thoughts and feelings by choosing your words carefully. You can also notice how your use of language gives clues to the way your perceptions of the world can be distorted by assumptions that you have made. For instance:

Shifting responsibility

A simple phrase like 'You make me sad' implies that one person can cause another to experience some emotion or inner state, leaving the person with no choice on how to respond. However, our thoughts and feelings happen within our own body and are the result of our perception of what is going on. So although someone else's behaviour may have triggered a perception, we are responsible for our inner response. It is worthwhile challenging such assumptions of cause and effect:

• You make me angry	What am I doing that causes you to feel angry?
• The work is frustrating	What is it about the work that you find frustrating?
• She confuses things	What are you confused about? How does she confuse you?

Mind reading

We often assume we know what's in someone else's mind without checking it out with them. This stems from the notion that basically everyone else thinks and feels like us. Here are some examples:

• My wife thinks I'm lazy	How do you know that is what she thinks?
• I know you're angry with me	What gives you the impression that I'm angry?
• He expects too much of me	What does he expect of you?

Putting it all together

At this early stage in the counselling process, you need to get as clear a picture as possible of how your own unique way of seeing the world is affecting your situation. If these ideas are new to you, it would be a good idea to practise using them. One way is to listen carefully to radio or television interviews, noticing how people might be indicating distortions or limits in their internal model. Ask a friend to make statements that contain one of the language patterns described, and then challenge each statement with the appropriate question.

EXERCISE

When you feel confident about using these ideas, take time to listen or read through the story you told. Notice whether there is consistent use of any of the patterns described, and begin to ask yourself the questions that a counsellor might ask. Be gentle with yourself – a counsellor wouldn't demand clarification or criticise your way of speaking. He or she would be encouraging you to explore your story with an attitude of interest rather than disapproval.

   If you are working with a partner or in a group, take it in turns to assume the role of counsellor, using the challenges to help clarify each person's story.

Reflection

The aim of this chapter was to guide you into the work of counselling. It has been concerned with laying out the facts of your situations and has introduced the idea of listening to what may lie under the surface language you use.

   This may have given you some important clues about where changes will be most effective. As before, take time to reflect on how you think and feel about the work of this session. Notice in particular any new thoughts which have occurred to you – it doesn't matter at this stage whether everything makes sense. That's fine – we are aiming to shake things up so that you can change the patterns with which you are unhappy. Things will fall into place in time. Chapter 4 will explore further ways in which you can make sense of what is happening.

4

The History

History teaches everything, even the future.

Alphonse de Lamartine

In the previous session, you focused on what is happening in your life at the moment. However, what has happened in the past may also be significant. Many counselling approaches encourage clients to look back into their history to help make sense of what is happening to them now. This chapter refers to some of the ideas developed by Eric Berne, the originator of Transactional Analysis (usually known as TA), to help you trace the significance of your own history. TA is a theory for understanding human relationships and offers a practical approach to changing the way we think, feel and behave.

There are several exercises in this chapter which ask you to remember your early childhood. Don't worry if you can't remember that far back. If you are interested in doing the exercises, you can use whatever knowledge you have about what things were like and make up what you think is most likely to have happened. If you are in contact with your parents, siblings or other important people who were around at that time, you can ask them for their memories. Not all counselling approaches place such importance on early memories, however, so if you prefer you can pass over these exercises and move on to the next stage.

Our life-script

Eric Berne believed that we begin writing our own life story at birth, the essentials of the plot being established about the time we are four and the story completed in all its main details around seven. Adolescence is the time for revising the story, testing out its main themes or, to quote Berne, 'putting the show on the road'.

As mentioned in Chapter 3, the degree to which our early history shapes our personality is open to question. As far as we know, our personality is the result of the intricate interplay between our genetically inherited traits and our experience of the environment into which we are born. The reason that many people seek counselling is that they want to change certain aspects of their personality which cause them a problem. This is often manifested in habitual behaviour which seems out of our control. Berne's ideas about how these habits originate gives us a workable way of identifying likely motives for the way we behave. For many people this is a crucial step towards making important changes.

Like all stories, our life-script has a beginning, middle and end; heroes, heroines, villains and bit-part players; a main theme and sub-plots. You may not be able to remember the beginnings of your story, but here are a few ways to trace some early decisions which became part of your script.

EXERCISE

Imagine that you have written the story which is your life. Write down the answers to the following questions, working quickly and accepting the first answers that come into your mind.

- What is the title of your story?
- What kind of story is it? Tragedy or comedy? Heroic or banal? Adventurous or boring?

- Who are the main characters? Is there a hero? A villain?
- How is the story likely to end?

Keep your answers because you may want to refer to them later.

In *What Do You Say After You Say Hello?* Berne defines a life-script as an ongoing plan developed in early childhood under parental influence, which directs the individual's behaviour in the most important aspects of his or her life. As you work through this chapter you will begin to appreciate how your life-script has developed and how it helps or hinders you through life.

A means of survival

Imagine that you are small and physically vulnerable, in a world populated by giants. You do not have the advantage of understanding the language and have no previous experience of life in this world. You are unable to make sense of what is happening because you cannot ask any questions or understand what is said to you. An unexpected noise, for instance, could signal danger. If you feel cold, you don't know how to warm up. If you are hungry, you have no idea where your next meal is coming from – or whether it is coming at all. This is just how it was when you were a baby.

The way to make a hostile environment feel safer is to make it predictable – that way we can prepare for and protect ourselves from danger. As babies, we can't think in adult ways. We sense the world through our emotions – feelings of rage, helplessness, happiness, fear. You have only to watch a baby to realise how intensely these feelings are experienced. As we struggle to create predictability by making sense of what is happening, we make early decisions about the nature of the world.

Consider a small child trying to make sense of having to go into hospital, being taken to an unfamiliar place, maybe separated from its parents, being in pain and handled by various strangers. There are a range of responses. The child might be sad that the predictable comfortable life experienced up to now has gone and wonder, 'Has it gone forever? Can I rely on anything lasting?' Alternatively he or she may feel fear and worry, 'What is going to happen? Will I ever survive?' Another response could be rage that the parents have let this happen: 'Aren't they supposed to keep life safe?' The child might even experience guilt: 'Has this happened to me because I am bad?'

Of course, if the grown-ups knew how the baby was responding they would try to explain. But how can you communicate the facts about a complex situation to someone who does not understand the language?

The child, trying to create some predictability, draws general conclusions from particular events. Decisions resulting from this stay in hospital might therefore run along the lines of 'You can't depend on people'; 'Life is full of pain'; 'There's something wrong with me'; 'I have to be brave and not show how I feel.'

This exercise in Script Analysis will help you identify early decisions of yours.

EXERCISE

You can use a tape recorder or paper and pen for this exercise. Give your responses to the questions fairly quickly. Trust your first response even if you are not sure what it may mean.

If you are working with a partner or a group, take it in turns to ask each other the questions. Record or note down the answers.

- What is your earliest memory?
- Is there a family story about your birth?
- What is the story about how you were named?
- Describe your mother.
- Describe your father.
- Describe yourself.
- What was your mother's main advice to you?
- What was your father's main advice to you?
- What did your mother want you to be?
- What did your father want you to be?
- What do you like most about yourself?
- Describe the good feeling that you most often have in your life.
- What could you do to make your mother angry?
- How did she express her anger? How did you respond?
- What could you do to make your father angry?
- How did he express his anger? How did you respond?
- What do you like least about yourself?
- Describe the bad feeling that you most often have in your life.
- What would 'heaven on earth' be for you?
- What do you wish your mother had done differently?
- What do you wish your father had done differently?
- If by magic you could change anything about yourself by just wishing, what would you wish for?
- What do you want most out of life?
- Do you think of yourself as a winner or a loser?
- How old will you be when you die?
- What will it say on your tombstone?

This script questionnaire will give important clues to the nature of your life-script. You may be able to see clear connections between your present ways of thinking, feeling and behaving and the early decisions you made.

Strokes and scripts

Eric Berne had another idea which underpins the life-script theory. He came across a well-known investigation undertaken in 1945 by a researcher called René Spitz, who observed babies brought up in a children's home. Although the children were looked after very well, they tended to experience more physical and emotional difficulties than children raised by their mothers or other direct carers. Spitz concluded that it was lack of stimulation and contact which affected the development of the babies from the children's home. It was from this and similar studies that the TA theory of strokes was developed. Berne chose the word 'stroke' to describe our infant need for touch. He felt that as grown-ups we still crave this contact because it lets us know that we exist. However, once we leave childhood we find ourselves in a society in which physical contact is strictly limited, and so we learn to substitute this need for other forms of recognition or strokes. A smile, a conversation or a compliment are all signs that we have been noticed.

Strokes can be experienced as pleasant or painful; verbal or non-verbal. Any contact we have with other people can be analysed in terms of strokes. You may see someone you know, smile and say, 'Hello'; they recognise you, smile back and reply, 'Hello, nice to see you.' This is a very simple stroke exchange; you have given each other positive recognition. On another occasion on meeting, you might smile and greet the person and be answered with a frown or an angry outburst. You won't feel great, but at least you have been acknowledged.

Berne felt that as infants we operated on the basis that any stroke is better than no stroke at all, and intuitive knowledge of our need for strokes led us to important script decisions. From our earliest moments, we test out all sorts of behaviours in order to find out how to get the strokes we need. When a particular form of behaviour succeeds, we are likely to repeat it and make a decision about it. In this way, strokes reinforce script decisions.

EXERCISE

Here is a list of things for which you might have got strokes while you were growing up. Mark each statement with a tick or a cross depending on whether the stroke was positive (praise, smiles, etc.) or negative (frowns, rebukes, etc.).

- For just being you – doing nothing in particular
- For being persistent
- For succeeding, being top, being first
- For being strong and independent; not relying on others
- For being funny and making people laugh
- For not making a fuss about problems
- For being caring and considerate of others
- For trying difficult tasks
- For being clumsy
- For making a mess
- For crying when you were frightened or sad
- For showing your anger
- For being quiet
- For saying 'no'
- For saying 'yes'
- For making a mistake
- For failing to finish a task
- For taking risks

- For being a leader
- For asking questions
- For doing things without being asked
- For hugging or kissing someone to show your affection
- For shouting
- For ???

You will find that all, some or none of these will apply to you. Add in as many of your own as you wish.

The value of this exercise is in any patterns that you can identify. Matters to think about, or to discuss with your partner or group, include:

- What is the balance between negative and positive strokes?
- Are any of the ways in which you were given positive or negative strokes in your childhood still important to you?
- Are any of the ways in which you got positive strokes in your childhood missing from your life now?
- Is there any way in which you are still seeking either positive or negative strokes which you experienced in your early life?

You can take this further if you wish, and analyse the way your stroke balance works for you. Berne identified four kinds of strokes:

- *Positive conditional:* 'That was a wonderful meal you cooked.'
- *Positive unconditional:* 'I love being with you.'
- *Negative conditional:* 'I don't like the way you've written this.'

- *Negative unconditional:* 'I dislike you.'

Notice that *unconditional* strokes are about what you are; *conditional* strokes are about what you do.

EXERCISE

Taking a recent ordinary day in your life, note down under the four headings any strokes you remember receiving; then note down the strokes you gave.

Once again, the importance is in any pattern you can detect. Do you, for instance, give more than you receive? Do you tend to receive (or give) only negative or conditional strokes? In building up a picture of your own stroke balance, you may see whether you need to make changes. If as a general rule you don't receive many positive strokes, think about how you can improve the situation. Similarly, if you've noticed that you tend not to give out positive strokes to others, you can deliberately set out to increase your output. Positive attention does make us feel better; when we feel good about ourselves we tend to be more effective in whatever we are doing; giving genuine positive strokes to others will make them feel valuable; when people feel valued they tend to be cooperative and accepting towards us. These are good reasons for developing positive stroke-giving habits.

EXERCISE

Identify forms of behaviour which would increase your positive stroke balance. For instance, if you want to give more positive strokes to others, note down a compliment which you could genuinely give to, say, five of your friends or family. If you want to receive more strokes, think of at least one thing you could ask

---

for from a friend or family member. Go ahead and give the compliments or ask for what you want.

Message received

It is important to remember that your script decisions resulted from your perception of what was going on around you. This perception was based on your infant ability to understand things, so it is possible that what you perceived was different from what was actually intended.

Even before you were able to speak you were interpreting messages through your experience of physical contact. If Mother held you closely and warmly you are likely to get the message, 'I'm loved and wanted.' If she was tense and worried – perhaps because she had never held a baby before – you might have decided, 'I'm unlovable and rejected.' The TA view is that these very early perceptions are extremely influential because they create the foundation from which other decisions are made.

Later on, as you began to understand language, even more messages were communicated. Perhaps you brought home the first painting you did at school. Here are some possible responses; notice how each one can send a powerful message which might lead to a script decision.

- Mother looks at the painting and says, 'What is that supposed to be? It's just a muddle.' (*Possible script decision: If I can't explain myself I won't be acceptable.*)
- Father picks up the painting, gives it a quick glance and puts it down without saying anything. (*Possible script decision: I'm not worth any attention.*)
- Mother smiles, looks at the painting, gives you a hug and pins the painting on the wall. (*Possible script decision: I'm loved and worthwhile.*)

- Father takes the painting, doesn't look at it but pats your head and laughs. (*Possible script decision: What I do isn't as important as how cute I am.*)
- Mother asks you how you did the painting and how you feel about it now. She gives you time to answer and listens to you carefully. (*Possible script decision: I can think; my thoughts matter.*)

EXERCISE

Refer to the script questionnaire and reflect on the kind of responses you remember getting from your parents and other adults to your early successes, failures, questions and ideas. Does this give you any clues about the kind of script you have? This is one of the exercises you can miss if you don't remember the details of your early childhood.

A blueprint for life

Script messages come in different forms. You may remember direct orders such as 'Don't be naughty'; 'Keep quiet'; 'Hurry up.' These instructions are about *doing* the right thing; others may be about *being* right: 'You're such a clever girl'; 'You're so clumsy'; 'You'll turn out just like Uncle Jim!' Another kind of message can be received by noticing how your parents talk about you. 'She's never going to make it'; 'He just won't take "no" for an answer'; 'She's so pretty.' The tone and body language which accompany these statements are also part of the communication.

These examples are verbal, but you are bound to have experienced non-verbal instruction as well. Being smacked or hugged are obvious examples, but there are more subtle lessons. Being ignored is a very potent message; a parent's silence can be more hurtful than a blow.

Geraldine was worried about her health. She was telling

the counsellor how, whenever things seemed to be going well, her health broke down. She told this story: 'I remember spending a whole morning making a cake for my Dad. I really wanted to please him. I iced it with a message: "I love you, Dad." I was very proud of it. I remember him coming into the kitchen; I'd left it on the table and I watched to see how he would react. He didn't even notice it. I felt demolished! I remember thinking, "What do I have to do to be noticed?"' Geraldine said he would be very attentive if she was ill. She identified the script decision, '*The only way I'll get what I need is to get ill.*' This doesn't mean her father wanted her to be ill – when a child decides it is with limited information. Maybe her father's attention was taken up with whatever problems he had at the time, or he just didn't know how to show affection. We can't know what was in his mind – all we do know is how Geraldine perceived the event. It also doesn't mean that her illnesses are not real. When she has a cold or flu the symptoms are genuine and incapacitating. But making this connection offers a way of making sense of what is happening.

Script no-no's

As therapists began using these ideas they found that, although their clients told different stories, certain themes emerged again and again. Bob and Mary Goulding identified commands or injunctions which many people pinpointed as being at the heart of their scripts.

Don't exist If you have ever thought of committing suicide or ever feel worthless, useless or unlovable, it may be that your script includes this injunction. Parents do sometimes say things like 'I could kill you for that!' or even 'I wish you'd never been born!' If these words confirm non-verbal signs given to you early in life, you can see how you might get the idea that you are not supposed to exist at all.

It is surprising how often the Don't Exist injunction

turns up in script analysis. Remember, though, that we are dealing with infant perceptions. A child can read all sorts of threats into behaviour which may to a grown-up appear quite harmless. A parent may easily say or do things in the heat of the moment which aren't really meant. A child might hear, 'If it weren't for you I could have gone to college/been able to travel....' and deduce that the parent really wishes the child was dead. The parent would be horrified to know the child thought that.

Don't be who you are is a variant of Don't Exist. It can be conveyed to a girl by parents who wanted a boy; to an artistic child by parents who wanted a sporty type; to a tall, straight-haired child by parents who wanted a small, dainty blonde. In later life this person might feel uncomfortable as the sex they are or the way they look, or try to succeed in a field for which they are not suited.

Don't feel means don't laugh, cry, be angry or scared when you feel like it. Sometimes there is a ban on a particular set of feelings in a family; feelings can be experienced but not shown. Boys are usually taught to hide their fear or hurt: 'Big boys don't cry!' Sometimes feelings are converted into action. If you are given food each time you feel bad, you might decide that eating is the only way to assuage painful feelings. Eating disorders or addictions are sometimes traced to this injunction.

Don't grow up ideas can arise from having a parent who loves babies but finds it difficult to relate to children as they grow up. People who have this in their script do find it hard to take adult responsibility.

Don't be close may be the message put across by parents who are afraid of the intensity of the child's feelings or who rarely touch each other or talk about their feelings. Or it may be the result of a parent leaving suddenly or dying.

The child might decide, 'There's no point in getting close to someone – they'll only leave me.' This is a script which can make it hard to maintain intimate relationships.

Don't think comes from a parent who consistently belittles the child. A child proudly explains something and is met by a laugh and a pat on the head; a clumsy attempt at a new task is taken over by the parent with impatience; a question is ignored; these are all ways in which the child might get the message that there's no point in thinking things out. As an adult, he or she will probably feel confused by thinking and discount his or her own abilities.

Don't Be Important; Don't Succeed; Don't Be Healthy; Don't Belong; Don't Grow Up are more messages that a child can collect.

EXERCISE

Read through the list of injunctions and notice any which have been important for you. You may be aware of different ones – if so, make your own list. Where do you think these ideas originated? From one particular parent? From things they said (or didn't say)? Things they did (or didn't do)? How do they affect you now?

What's the use of knowing the script?

You can think of your script as a plan of action, a map of life you created a long time ago to help you navigate through a territory you didn't understand. Scripts come in all shapes and sizes: short and sweet like *Cinderella*, and long and tortuous like *Anna Karenina*. It is useful to have identified the key areas of your script because you will have important clues as to why your life takes the turns it does.

Reflection

Look at what you have gathered from the exercises in this chapter. Think or talk over what you have discovered so far. Are you happy with the script you seem to have? Are there any parts you would like to change? Remember *you* are the writer; although others were instrumental in the decisions you made, you are now grown up enough to make better sense of the world and to make decisions based on your new understanding.

Your stroke balance, which you explored in this chapter, can be increased through self-stroking. Many of us have grown up with the belief that giving ourselves positive attention is the slippery slope to self-satisfaction and smugness. So we developed the ability to ignore or even belittle our achievements. It is true that someone who only talked about how wonderful they were would become very boring and not at all popular, but that is a far cry from spending a little time every now and again to stock up on some positive strokes that you can give yourself. This reflection time is a good opportunity to give yourself some strokes. Here is one idea:

EXERCISE

On a large sheet of paper write down everything good that you know about yourself. Take your time, and then put up the paper where you can see it.

Counselling focuses on the problem areas of life, but this exercise will help you keep a sense of perspective, reminding you of your good qualities and what you have achieved. These resources are what will help you achieve even more, so it's important to keep sight of them.

In Chapter 5 you will move away from your past towards whatever it is in the present which is causing you problems.

5

Here and Now

The present is the necessary product of all the past.

Robert Green Ingersoll, 1833–99

Interesting and illuminating as the past can be, it isn't wise to stay in it forever. However angry or sad thinking about it makes you feel, you won't be able to change anything about it. It is the present and the future with which you are concerned now. In this chapter, therefore, we will explore an approach called Gestalt, largely the work of Fritz Perls. He felt that you could spend too long contacting repressed memories and experiences from the past and that it could be just as valuable to focus on the present, which he called the *here and now*.

Raising our awareness

Although we are always living in the present moment, you might be surprised how little we are aware of all that is actually happening. The following exercises are designed to demonstrate the point.

EXERCISE

Sit quietly for five minutes with your eyes closed. Just focus on listening and notice how many sounds you can hear.

Before you continue, reflect on this experience of listening. How many sounds came into your consciousness as time went on? For instance, you may have become aware of the sound of your heart beating, or of your own breathing; of distant birdsong or traffic; of a clock ticking. These sounds were going on all the time out of your awareness. The pace of modern living makes it hard to be conscious of everything around us and we can be very cut off from the richness of the environment. The next exercises continue this theme.

EXERCISE

Look around the room, noticing the shapes, colours, forms and textures that you can see. Relax your eyes and let things go out of focus. Try to see as a visitor from Mars might see things. The Martian wouldn't know the name or the purpose of anything. He wouldn't be able to make judgements like something being in the right place; dirty or clean; old or new. Try looking at just one object for at least five minutes and notice whether it (or your view of it) changes as time passes.

Spend five minutes walking around the room, touching as many textures as possible. You can do this blindfold if you wish.

Take some food – a piece of fruit, a biscuit or a salad vegetable – and eat it very slowly. Keeping your eyes closed, concentrate on the taste, the feel of the food in your mouth, the rhythm of your chewing, etc.

Now, still with your eyes closed, concentrate on your sense of smell. What does the air smell like? Smell your hand, the wall, the open window, the different objects around you.

Those exercises were concerned with raising awareness of your senses; now experiment with your mental awareness.

EXERCISE

Sit quietly with a notebook and pen and allow your thoughts to wander. Don't think about anything in particular. Set a timer for ten minutes so that you don't have to worry about the time. Every time a thought comes to you, however trivial, jot it down.

When the time is up, look over your list and notice the pattern of your thinking. Are your thoughts largely concerned with the past or with the future? Are you judging or criticising yourself or others most of the time? Did your thoughts flit from one thing to another, or did you focus on one main issue? Thoughts can be helpful or hindering. For instance, I could be writing this and thinking, 'Am I going to meet the deadline? Will people understand what I'm saying? Some people are bound to disagree with me. When shall I cook dinner?' These thoughts could easily block the flow – it would be wiser just to get on with it and meet any problems if or when they arise.

EXERCISE

You have concentrated on your senses and your mind; now is time to focus your attention on your body. Again, sit quietly and take stock of your physical self. Are you aware of any aches and pains? Is your posture straight or slumped? Are your muscles relaxed or tense?

The purpose of all these exercises has been to raise your awareness of your own particular here and now. Awareness of this kind can help us recognise how we may be restricting our responses and how we can act to change. Just as we successfully screen out many sights and sounds from our consciousness, so we filter our awareness of the options open to us. For instance, we can immobilise ourselves by avoiding awareness of what we don't like in our present situation. We can tune out recognition of our own needs and tune into the needs of others. Perls encouraged people to be fully present, to become aware of their current needs, to take responsibility for themselves and their actions. He emphasised the importance of rounding off unfinished situations to make a whole: it is important to deal fully with a situation in the present so that it does not block our ability to move on. This process of completing 'unfinished business' involves filling out gaps in our awareness.

Controlling our responses to life

This focus on awareness of your own needs isn't as selfish as it sounds – being aware of a need doesn't mean that you automatically have the right to fulfil it at the expense of other people. Bringing this knowledge into consciousness gives you more control over the way you respond to life.

Take Caroline, for example, who joined the Parent Teacher Association of the school that her daughter attended. When she went to her first meeting, she felt uncomfortable. Everyone else appeared to know what to do, and they all seemed to know each other whereas she knew no one because the family had only just moved into the area. She felt awkward, unsure where to sit, whether to take her coat off or not, not knowing when or if she would have a chance to ask any questions. So she sat right at the back of the room, not speaking to anyone and feeling more and more out of place. She thought it was inevitable that she should feel this way – she was a shy person and always felt this way in a group.

Inclusion, control and affection

However, she could experience this event in a different way. William Schutz is a psychologist who studied people's behaviour in groups. He recognised that people seemed to be influenced by three very basic needs which he called *inclusion*, *control* and *affection*. How we behave in order to meet these largely unconscious needs is an important element in our script. To be included is something that most of us want to some extent or other; it is as if we ask ourselves, 'What do I have to do to be liked/appreciated/recognised/accepted in this group?' and then behave according to the answer we give. For some people the issue is more about how much they can be in control. For them the questions are, 'How much will I be in charge of what happens to me? Who looks like they will want to control me? Whom will I be able to control?' Affection is to do with our need for intimate contact with others. At some time in the life of every group, certain people will create close friendships with one or two others.

Caroline, with her high inclusion and affection needs, wants people to accept and like her but is afraid that if she does the wrong thing they won't. Her fear paralyses her, and so she does nothing. Her disquiet comes from the conflict thrown up by her own needs. You may remember from Chapter 4 that we create our script very early in life – long before we can rationally assess the best way to deal with what is happening. Caroline's script believes that the best way to deal with the fear of rejection is to be quiet and good, so that is what she is doing at the meeting. By seeing the situation in this way, Caroline can understand that her reaction to the PTA meeting really comes from the past, when her efforts to be accepted may well have met with rejection. Now that she is grown up, though, her wellbeing does not depend on being accepted by this particular group of people. She has questions to ask and information to gather. Sitting at the back of the room and being a 'good girl' is not likely to help her succeed. She can use her awareness to help overcome her fear and react more rationally to the 'here and now'.

The figure and the ground

Perls, interested in why people so often seemed to act in ways which ensured that their apparent needs would not be met, used the terms *figure* and *ground* as a way of explaining how our unconscious survival needs, such as inclusion, control and affection, take precedence over those which are conscious. The way we learn to organise our behaviour to fulfil these needs becomes so routine that we don't think about it. Caroline, for instance, isn't thinking, 'Because I feel I won't survive if people don't accept me, I'm going to keep very quiet so that no one has the chance to reject me.' Her thoughts run along the lines: 'These people are so unfriendly. Why don't they make it easy for me? I just can't cope with crowds.'

So at this moment her need to survive is the figure and dominates her behaviour; if that need gets met it will recede into the ground and another need will come to the fore. If she feels more comfortable and accepted, she might feel brave enough to ask her questions. Her need for information becomes the figure and she acts to meet it.

Investigating 'here and now' behaviour

Perls felt that all our behaviour – the way we talk, breathe, move, laugh, censor, scorn, look for causes and so on – is the expression of our dominant needs. So examining our behaviour in minute detail raises awareness of those needs. Counsellors using Gestalt techniques are very interested in the minutiae of 'here and now' behaviour – often focusing on a body movement, a word, a particular phrase or breathing pattern to try to understand the motivation for self-defeating patterns of behaviour. The following exercises will give you a taste of this kind of investigation.

EXERCISE

Think of a recent situation when you were not getting what you wanted. These questions will help you identify which needs you were meeting:

- What thoughts went through your mind during the event you have chosen?
- Which of these thoughts were related to the actual event? Which were familiar thoughts about yourself?
- What feelings did you experience?
- How were the feelings relevant to what was actually happening?
- Did you experience any physical sensations (e.g. blushing, tension, pain?)
- Are these sensations familiar? Did they help or hinder you at the time?
- What did you actually do?
- Looking back, did your actions help you meet your objectives? If not, what needs do you think they could possibly have been meeting?

The Gestalt approach to counselling places great emphasis on taking responsibility for yourself, which means being willing to be accountable for everything you think, feel and do. This means you need to accept that, whatever other people seem to be doing to you, your response happens in your mind and body and arises from your perception of the situation. It is the willingness to accept this 'response-ability' that helps you to make changes.

The language of self-responsibility

In Chapter 1 we explored the importance of using language to communicate our thoughts and feelings truthfully. Language can also help trigger awareness of how we may be avoiding this level of responsibility. Gaie Houston, a therapist and teacher of Gestalt, adapted the ideas of an American psychologist called John Weir who became frustrated with English as a language for communicating accurately what goes on in people's inner world. He introduced modifications which reflect the principle of self-responsibility and which we can call Responsibility Language. There are a few basic rules, the first of which relates to the many ways we can talk about our experience without using the word 'I'.

Do you remember Caroline at the PTA meeting? She is thinking to herself, 'These people are making me feel awkward. How can someone as shy as me be expected to do anything but wait to be noticed?' In Responsibility Language she would say, 'I am making me feel awkward. I'm using my shyness to avoid doing anything. I'm choosing to wait to be noticed.' You can see how Responsibility Language keeps Caroline as the subject of her experience and points to the way in which she herself is contributing to the problem. Here are some more examples:

Conventional English	*Responsibility Language*
My bad temper gets me into trouble	I make me angry; I get me into trouble
You make me sad/ angry/happy	I make me sad/angry/ happy
An idea just came to me	I made me think....
That's frustrating	I make me frustrated
You're confusing me	I am confusing myself with your words
I don't know what to say	I don't know how to say the thoughts in my mind
It doesn't matter	I don't matter

These all show how we distance ourselves from responsibility for our thoughts, feelings and actions by the language we use. 'My bad temper gets me into trouble' implies that 'my bad temper' is separate from 'me' and is causing the trouble. 'You're confusing me' implies that the fact I don't understand is your fault.

When you next hear yourself or anyone else around you using the words 'this', 'you', 'that', 'what', or 'it', experiment with changing the sentence to use 'I' instead. Conventional English is marvellous for describing one's outer reality; Responsibility Language focuses on the inner experience – what you are actually doing from moment to moment.

Another important rule of Responsibility Language is related to the role of the word 'you'. If I say, 'You've just had your hair cut', my meaning is probably clear. Everyone can see the length and style of your hair. On the other hand, if I say, 'You are so lazy!' there is less likely to be agreement. You may know that you have in fact been working extremely hard for the last year and have decided to rest for a while. Others may know you as very careful or conscientious or depressed or anxious or whatever. Each 'you' is the product of every individual's perception. John Weir suggested that we could acknowledge this by talking about 'the you-in-me', thus taking responsibility for our own perceptions and assumptions. 'You are so lazy' becomes 'The you-in-me is so lazy', which sounds rather strange but highlights the point that I am talking about my perception of you which is based on my expectations. These two rules change a simple phrase such as 'I love you' to 'I make me love the you-in-me'! More examples:

Conventional Language	*Responsibility Language*
You make me angry	I make myself angry with the you-in-me
You make me happy	I am happy with the you-in-me
You don't care about me	The you-in-me doesn't care

EXERCISE

Take each sentence in turn and translate it into Responsibility Language. As well as writing them down, try speaking the words and notice any difference you experience.

- This Responsibility Language is very difficult.
- I'm too stupid to understand it.
- It doesn't make sense
- You're much more able than I am to understand this.

- It's very confusing.
- It's beginning to make sense.

Here are some other rules and exercises for you to try:

But/and

EXERCISE

Make a series of statements each with the word 'but' in the middle. What effect does the 'but' have upon the statement? Usually 'but' kills whatever went before. 'You've done really well this year, but what a pity you made that mistake.' Repeat the statements and replace each 'but' with 'and'. Does this change anything?

Can't/won't

Each time you say 'I can't ....' you imply that there is some force outside yourself stopping you – that you would do it if you could.

EXERCISE

Make a series of statements beginning 'I can't...'; then repeat these saying exactly what you said before except for changing 'I can't...' to 'I won't...'. Be aware of how you experience each sentence. Is this something really impossible – or is it something possible that you refuse to do? Become aware of your capability and your power of refusal.

I need/I want

Needs are things we feel driven by and can't survive without. However, there is a difference between something that you really need, such as food and water, and other things you want that are very pleasant but not absolutely necessary. It might be truer to say, for instance, 'I want you to stay with me because I am afraid of being lonely' rather than 'I need you to stay'.

***

EXERCISE

Make a series of statements beginning 'I need...'; now repeat, replacing 'I need...' with 'I want...'. Take time to experience each sentence. Is this something you really need, or is it something that you want but could easily survive without?

***

I have to/I choose to

Realise that you do have the power of choice, even if it is the choice between two undesirable alternatives: 'I choose to stay with my job because I feel more secure that way' rather than 'I have to stay with my job.'

***

EXERCISE

As in previous exercises, make statements beginning with the words 'I have to...' and then repeat them, replacing 'I have to...' with 'I choose to...'. Notice what you experience; maybe you sense the beginning of taking responsibility for your choices.

***

I'm afraid to/I would like to

Fear often stops us even thinking about something that we want.

EXERCISE

List all the things you are afraid to try and then repeat the list, prefacing each item with the words 'I would like to...'. This change of phrase allows you to explore attractions and risks, potential losses and gains so that you can make a conscious choice rather than one ruled by fear.

'I have to', 'I can't', 'I need' or 'I'm afraid to' all imply that you have no choices – but in fact you are always making choices. Changing your language helps you get in touch with the hidden choices you are making now. Then you can begin to explore the possibilities of other choices.

EXERCISE

Take the example of a relationship which you are not happy with at the moment. Write or record a description of it as if you were talking directly to the other person involved, speaking straight from your heart. When you have finished, read or listen to what you have said.

Now translate it into Responsibility Language, using the rules described above.

Edward, whose relationship with his partner was breaking down, wrote, 'I get hurt when you ignore me. You make me angry because you never think of what I need. I'm afraid to tell you how I feel because you might leave. I can't understand why you want to make me so unhappy.'

His rewritten version was, 'I hurt myself when the you-in-me ignores me. I make me angry because the you-in-me never thinks of what I want. I want to tell you how I feel and I've made myself afraid that you might choose to leave me. I won't understand why the you-in-me wants me unhappy.' The exercise triggered three new thoughts for Edward. The first was how he had been blaming his partner without exploring how and why he was reacting in that particular way; the second that he was reacting to his *beliefs* about his partner as if they were *truths*; and the third that he was not being deprived by his partner of anything he *needed* – he could survive without her if necessary.

Paying attention to the language you are using is one way to keep you in touch with the 'here and now'. Here are some other experiments you can try.

Fitting the puzzle together

The word 'Gestalt' means a 'whole' brought together from split pieces. You could think of it in terms of a jigsaw puzzle with many pieces. Some of them fit together nicely; some need to be turned over; some don't seem to fit anywhere; some seem to be missing altogether.

Perls created a three-zone model to explain how we managed the split between our conscious and unconscious. Imagine for a moment that you have been thwarted in some way and are raging inside. This is your natural reaction – you in your 'inner zone'. Suppose, though, you were constantly criticised for this kind of reaction. Perhaps at some stage in your early life a parent stood over you and told you that nobody would love you if you were angry. You may have got the message that to be acceptable you would always have to be calm and 'well-behaved'. So your 'middle zone' is full of instructions like 'keep smiling', 'don't stamp your feet', 'Swallow your anger', 'Be good' and so on. Your response is filtered through this middle zone, and by the time it gets to the 'outer zone' you are able to deny that the anger has anything to do with you at all.

Learning to explore and communicate emotions is not easy, and we often stop ourselves by obeying those middle zone voices. You will avoid this if you:

- stay aware of what is happening in your mind and body;
- stay in the present rather than with memories of the past or fantasies about the future;
- realise that your *thoughts* and *feelings* aren't right or wrong in themselves. You should certainly judge our (and other people's) *behaviour*, but being truly aware of how you are reacting will give you useful clues towards understanding yourself more fully.

If you try to avoid a feeling, it doesn't go away but it hangs around and pops up again and again. A Gestalt counsellor is likely to say to their client, 'Can you stay with this feeling?', believing that the best way to deal with painful or unpleasant feelings is to work through them rather than dismiss them.

Repairing the splits

Gestalt, you will remember, means a 'whole' brought together from split parts. An important part of the therapeutic process is to bring these parts together.

For instance, we have a way of avoiding any distasteful or unacceptable aspects of ourselves by 'projecting' them on to other people. We can then ignore, avoid or criticise them, while continuing to remain unchanged ourselves. So if you criticise someone for being deceitful, in Gestalt practice you are encouraged to act the role of a deceitful person. If there is someone you don't like you might be prompted to play their part, talking as if you were them and imagining being inside their skin.

EXERCISE

Conjure up an image of someone whom you find diffi-cult to get on with. When you can see him or her clearly in your mind, imagine that you have become this person. Imagine speaking, standing, laughing, working, sitting as they do. When you have finished, think about your experience. How easy did you find this mental role-play? Did you find yourself actually enjoying acting as the other person? Is there anything of this person in you?

The theory is that exploring matters which cause us some kind of problem allows us to check whether we are project-ing some part of ourselves on to the person. If we are, we can take responsibility for the projection and change our response as a result.

Perls pointed out that we can experience splits within ourselves. We say things like, 'My backache is getting on top of me' – as if 'me' and the 'backache' are completely separate. Once again we can separate the splits and, by exploring them, bring them together.

Our bodies are responding to the environment all the time. When we are in pain our natural impulse seems to be to cover it up as much as we can. However, pain does not just arrive out of the blue; it can only be the result of some-thing which is happening. An organ may be mal-functioning; muscles may be tense in response to anger or fear; the immune system may not be working well. Whatever the reason, the function of the symptom is to alert us to what is happening in our body. The following Gestalt exercise is useful if you are currently suffering from some physical pain. It won't magically cure the symptom but it may well raise your awareness to any connection with what is generally happening in your life.

EXERCISE *Conversation with a Symptom:*

Settle down comfortably and focus on some part of your body which is causing you discomfort or pain. Use your imagination to visualise this symptom and give yourself time to explore the image you create. You might choose to draw a picture or, if you are working with someone else, to describe it.

Imagine that you can ask the symptom questions and that it can answer. Ask what function it is carrying out for you and listen to the answer. Now imagine that you are this symptom; allow yourself to experience what it feels like; what you think about the body you are in; whether you have anything to say.

Then imagine that you become yourself again and notice whether your image of the symptom has changed in any way.

Frances tried this exercise by focusing on her headache. The image which came to her was a dense cloud filling up her head. 'It's like a blanket obscuring my thoughts. The cloud is very dark, swirling about, and every now and again there is a flash like lightning. The flashes seem to get right inside me with a sharp pain.' She imagined herself asking this cloud what it was doing. 'I'm forcing you to stop thinking. I'm tired of trying to be perfect and being criticised all the time.' She imagined herself as the cloud: 'I'm swirling about; I feel all over the place; I can't decide where to settle. This head I'm in is too full, too busy – so I've got to keep moving about. I want to rest.' Frances knew that she was working under extreme pressure and that her stress was increased because she was highly critical of herself. She realised that it was important for her to relax and give herself a rest. This did not miraculously cure the headache, but the exercise made her mindful of the need to look after herself better. As she did so, the headaches diminished.

The 'bodytalk' exercise is an example of how to stay with what is actually happening, even if it is painful or difficult. The aim of counselling is to understand oneself more fully, and so it is important to stay with what you are feeling and thinking rather than to pretend nothing is happening.

Conversations with cushions and empty chairs

Another kind of split which we can try to repair is what Gestalt therapists call 'unfinished business'. As we go through life there are likely to be many times when we aren't able to complete a relationship satisfactorily. When we feel that someone is mistreating us we are bound to have a reaction, but for many reasons we may not communicate it. Feelings of anger, fear, frustration, sadness or guilt seem to lodge in our unconscious, affecting us in ways we have already discussed. Another possibility is that we carry sadness and guilt because someone who is important to us died before we could communicate good feelings like love and affection.

A typical Gestalt practice is to encourage people to complete such situations by imagining the person with whom the communication is unfinished and speaking to them. If there is someone in your life with whom you have unfinished business, try the following exercise:

EXERCISE

Set up your room so that you are sitting opposite an empty chair or floor cushion. Imagine the person to whom you want to speak sitting in the chair, and tell

---

them the things you want them to hear. When you
have finished, you can move to the empty chair yourself and take on the role of the other person. Let them
speak through you; the response may be very
predictable, or you may be surprised by what you say
or feel. Let the conversation continue until you are
satisfied that you have said all you wish.

Then sit quietly and reflect on any insight that this
exercise has given you.

The Gestalt empty chair can be a powerful device which
enables you to discharge long-stored feelings. The theory is
that the energy being used to control these reactions
connected with the past can be released for more creative
purposes.

In Gestalt counselling, the empty chair or cushion can be
used for acting out any internal split. For instance, often
our head and our heart are responding very differently to a
situation. By giving each a voice, you can use your energy to
make the best decision rather than keeping one or other
voice down. This technique is probably going to seem artificial or silly at first; you may feel stilted and awkward
speaking in ways which are unfamiliar. It is a useful device,
though, for exploring the contradictions or conflicts which
we experience.

Mental dogfights

Perls often described inner conflicts as the fight between 'top
dog' and 'underdog'. This could be described as the conflict
between our conscience (the 'top dog') and our innermost
desires ('underdog'). Top dog is often the louder voice,
telling us what we 'should/must/ought' to do. 'Underdog' is
the opposing voice, expressing what we want or need. A
typical dialogue between them might run as follows:

Top Dog	*Underdog*
• You should work harder	I'm fed up with working so hard
• You must control your eating	One chocolate won't do me any harm
• Do what you're told	I'll do what I like

When these voices are in conflict, we tend to assume that one must be right and the other wrong. This leads us to expend much energy in either subduing the underdog or ignoring the top dog. The Gestalt idea is to give equal voice to both, because our personality contains both and each is valuable. We would then be in a better position to make a rational decision about the wisest thing to do, taking both into account. We can make a better match between doing the right thing with regard to our responsibilities to others and society in general, and our deepest wishes. Not to do this can leave us with the choice of rebelling for the sake of it in order to give ourselves the fantasy of freedom, or suppressing our own wants and needs entirely. It was Perls' belief that if we constantly deny acknowledgement of our desires, they will show themselves in some way – often through body language of which we are largely unconscious.

EXERCISE

If you are finding it difficult to make a decision, or are facing a conflict of some sort, you could set up a top dog/underdog dialogue. Arrange two chairs facing each other, one to represent the top dog and the other underdog. Sit in the one which seems the stronger at the moment, and give voice to all the thoughts and feelings which come up. Then move to the other chair and give voice to those thoughts and feelings. If you are doing the exercise on your own you would find it very interesting to tape your dialogue.

Reflection

In this chapter the spotlight has been on you in the 'here and now'. The Gestalt approach emphasises the importance of facing yourself as you are, warts and all. All the exercises encourage awareness of the present, helping you to become more aware of your body sensations, emotions, behaviour and the choices you are making in your life. It is as if you are able to meet each different part of yourself, positive and negative, with a view to understanding how each contributes to your whole personality. Concentrating on the minutiae of everyday language and behaviour gives you a way of exploring in detail the patterns of tension which may be blocking you from expressing feelings directly. Before you move on, take some time to reflect on what you have learned so far. In Chapter 6 we will be looking even further into the problems you may be experiencing, in order to find new ways of thinking and responding to what is happening.

6

A New Angle

There's more than one way to skin a cat.

Traditional proverb

This proverb was never brilliant news for cats, but makes a good opening for this chapter. The point of the work we have done so far is to help you develop a deeper understanding of the problems you may be facing. You have delved into memories of the past as well as analysing what you are doing now to give you a deeper insight into patterns which could be hindering you. Sometimes this level of understanding is enough to point the way forward – but if it isn't, we need to move on. The best course of action may not yet be obvious; however, it is probably clear that whatever you are doing at the moment is not working as well as you want. So it is time to think about doing something else.

To do so, you need a new way of seeing things. Not changing your present perspective means that you are likely to stay in the same place. If you wear spectacles, you will know what happens when they need changing. For some time you may not even notice that you can't see as clearly as before; you have got used to distorted vision. Then, when you get a new pair of glasses, you see things very differently. This is the kind of change for which we are aiming.

New outlooks lead to new action by challenging old perspectives. Take the case of Georgina, a law student who wanted to be a writer. She had great success with her writing while she was at college, making quite a name for herself editing the college magazine. She decided to leave college before she qualified so that she could work on the novel she was writing. She could not understand why her family and friends were doubtful about the wisdom of her decision. They were not so sure that she had the talent to succeed immediately in the competitive publishing world. She went to see the college counsellor, who challenged her to obtain an informed evaluation of her present work by sending it to publishers and agents. Georgina did so and was surprised by the lack of enthusiasm shown by those whom she had approached. She did get valuable feedback which would help to sharpen her work, but it was clear that it would not be as easy as she thought to make her way as an author. She decided to stay at college, finish her course and consider her future more carefully.

The counsellor challenged Georgina's belief that her success at college automatically meant that she would be successful in the world outside – not by telling her she was wrong, but by inviting her to test it out. She did not give up the idea of writing, but decided to create a more secure employment base for herself first.

If you have been trying to change things in your life for some time but without success, use the work in this chapter to find ways of challenging yourself to think differently.

Challenge your beliefs

You will know from previous chapters that you can use the 'map' of beliefs you created from your childhood experiences to give meaning to present-day behaviour. Sometimes it is these very beliefs which are preventing change, and it is worth challenging these ideas and finding other ways of thinking about the situation.

EXERCISE

Focus on something that you would like to change about yourself or your life. Write the words 'I believe that ...' on a sheet of paper and list all the ways you can finish that sentence. Repeat the exercise completing the following:

- I believe that ... (write the name of each person close to you who may be affected by the change you want to make – family, friends, work colleagues, etc. This space is for any thoughts, feelings, beliefs or actions which you think they have about the change you want to make.)
- I believe that the world ...

If you are working on your own, finish the whole exercise and then read over what you have written. If there are any statements of fact, check if you have them right. If you have included opinions about your or other people's abilities, thoughts or intentions, check what evidence you have to support your statements.

If you are working in a group or with a partner, you can take it in turns to complete the sentences verbally. When you take the 'listener' role, don't interrupt until the speaker has finished. Then, gently go over each item in the list, asking 'What is your evidence for ...?

Harry had been trying to give up smoking for years. He tried all sorts of methods but always ended up smoking again. His lists looked like this:

I believe that:

- I'll never have the will power to give up
- giving up smoking is difficult for everyone

- smoking is bad for me
- I'll get depressed if I give up
- I'll put on weight
- I'll never find anything else to take the place of cigarettes
- I really want to give it up
- It is 'manly' to smoke

I believe that Marion (his wife) and the kids:

- want me to stop
- don't really understand how hard it is
- don't know how to help me do it
- think that I'm weak

I believe that the world:

- is so stressful that I need cigarettes to get me through each day
- thinks that smoking is less dangerous than other drugs

He explored the belief that he couldn't give up because (a) he would never have the willpower and (b) he would feel so terrible that it wouldn't be worth it. It was true that he had not succeeded so far, but he had no evidence that he could not succeed in the future. He spoke to people who had given up and found that, while some had indeed had a bad time, others had experienced no problem at all. He needed to challenge his assumption that he would belong to the 'bad time' group. He also though about his belief that he wanted to give up and realised that, while he did want to give up taking the risks that smoking carried with it, his smoking fulfilled certain needs. In order for him to succeed, those needs would have to be fulfilled some other way.

He also checked out his assumptions about his family's attitude. He realised that, if it was true that they didn't understand how hard it was, it was because he had never discussed it with them.

Finally, he decided that, whatever the world seemed to believe, he did not have to subscribe to those beliefs which were harmful for him.

Challenging his beliefs gave Harry a new perspective on the problem. He saw that, if he wanted to succeed, he would have to take more control over his thinking and more responsibility for his actions. He realised with a clarity which had been missing before that only *he* could stop him smoking!

Changing roles

Challenging your beliefs gives you a new frame of reference. Janet had been married for eight years when she began to feel dissatisfied. This is how she first expressed her unhappiness: 'I try my best to make Ken happy, but he's never satisfied with anything I do. He expects me to be at his beck and call and then criticises me for not enjoying myself enough. We always do what he wants to do. Sometimes I'd like to do things on my own or with a friend, but he says that's unreasonable. I don't like to argue but it's getting me down. I am very unhappy.'

With the aim of helping Janet to widen her perceptions, the counsellor suggested that she took on the role of Ken for a while, pretending that he had listened to what had just been said. As Ken, Janet said, 'I know Janet's unhappy, but whenever I ask her what the matter is she says, "Nothing." It's true we have different tastes, but since she never says what she wants I think I might as well go ahead and do what I want. At least I know what it is.'

When Janet had finished speaking as Ken, she was silent for a while and then said, 'That's true, you know. I don't tell him – I think that if he loved me enough he would know what I wanted. I can see that I'm responsible for a lot of

how I feel. If I was clearer about what I wanted, I can see we
might argue over differences – but we would be communicating. I know that I'm afraid of getting into arguments,
perhaps because my parents were always fighting when I
was little. I don't want my marriage to be like theirs, but I
think that if I go on like this it will be like theirs – not so
noisy but just as unhappy!'

As a result of this role-playing exercise, Janet started to
realise how her old belief system was creating problems.
One of those beliefs was that if she put forward needs which
differed from Ken's they would argue and end up like her
parents. Now she is beginning to understand how the
behaviour she thought was a solution to the problem was
actually contributing to her unhappiness. She had never
thought of things in this way before; up to now she had felt
that Ken was entirely to blame. Once she could see that the
responsibility for the relationship was shared, she could
think about changes she might want to make to improve
things.

EXERCISE

Trying to get inside someone else's 'skin' is a very
good way of seeing a situation from a different angle. If
there is someone with whom you are having difficulties at the moment, imagine that you are this person.
This might seem more difficult than it actually is.
Take your time with the exercise. Start by visualising
the person in your mind and then speak as you know
they do. It is like playing a part in a play – and you are
writing the script. Pretend to be him or her and write
or say how you see the situation from your (the other
person's) point of view. You might set up a dialogue
between you as 'you' and you as 'the other'. Take
plenty of time to think over any new thoughts that this
exercise raises.

Don't defeat yourself

Albert Ellis, another American psychologist, believed that there were some very common self-defeating beliefs which would get in the way of effective living. Here are some examples:

- I must always have the love and approval of all the important people in my life.
- It's not worth doing something unless I can do it well.
- My plans must always work out.
- People who harm me should be blamed and punished because they are bad.
- I must keep myself safe from danger, and if I am in danger at any time I must be anxious and fearful.
- I should not have problems, and if I do then I should be able to solve them quickly and painlessly.
- Other people or outside influences are responsible for anything that goes wrong in my life, so I cannot be expected to take responsibility for how I feel.
- It's easier to avoid life's difficulties than to face them.
- The past is to blame for how I am now.
- Passivity will protect me from danger.

If you recognise any of these, think carefully about how true they really are and how they could be replaced with more reasonable beliefs. For instance, 'I must always have the love and approval of all the important people in my life' could become 'I would like to be loved and approved of by those people who are important, but I know I can survive without it.' 'My plans must always work out' could become 'My plans may work out; if they don't I will deal with the situation as and when it becomes necessary.'

Reframe the problem

Sometimes the way we state our problems keeps us stuck in them. Restating a seemingly insoluble problem as solvable can be like shining a light into a dark hole. For instance you might find yourself saying something like, 'It doesn't matter how hard I try to change things – basically my life is a disaster. There's no way I can become successful. My early life was unhappy. My parents split up in a very hostile way. We kept on moving because we had no money. If things had been easier for me then I wouldn't have so many difficulties now. I'm just unlucky.'

Stated in that way, things certainly do seem to be pretty bad and it's difficult to see a way out. Supposing, though, you looked at things in this way: 'Ever since my childhood, which was unhappy, I have been blaming my parents for not giving me the love I needed. There was nothing I could do at the time to change things, and I did the best I could to survive. Now, though, I'm still letting this affect how I live my life. I avoid making close relationships because I'm afraid they will turn out like my parents' did. I don't stretch myself in my job because I'm sure I will fail. I spend more time thinking about how things were bad in the past than I do about what I could do with my life in the future. I want to loosen the chains of the past so that I can be free to be myself.' By thinking in this way, you would be distinguishing between what your parents were responsible for and what you are responsible for. It is true that you cannot change the past – but you can take control of the future.

EXERCISE

If you have a problem which seems to have no solution, experiment with this exercise to help you see things differently. Write out your own problem and

---

then reframe it in the style of the example. The Gestalt exercises on Responsibility Language (see pp. 73–6) might be useful here.

Finding a metaphor can be a good way of thinking differently. What metaphor best describes your life at the moment? Here are some examples:

- A jigsaw puzzle with some of the pieces turned over, some which don't seem to fit anywhere, some bits of the picture completed. The big problem is that I don't have the box with a picture to follow!
- My life is just like a poker game. Sometimes I'm dealing, sometimes I'm dealt to. The game needs luck and skill. Sometimes I don't even know what cards I'm holding; mostly other people seem to be winning!
- I feel like I'm in a long corridor with lots of doors on each side. Some are open and I know what would await me if I went through them. Others are closed but I could just push them open. Yet others are locked and I don't have a key.

If you have come up with a metaphor, can you use the images to give you ideas about how to proceed?

You are not alone

Most counsellors challenge their clients from time to time, especially if they can see how they are unwittingly contributing to their problems. Counsellors have the advantage of being completely objective because they are uninvolved in the client's life. They have no vested interest in hanging on to old perceptions and patterns. If you are working through this book on your own, this stage might be hard to do by yourself. However open you might be to challenge yourself, there's no way you can be as objective and uninvolved as a counsellor. Even though you may be reading this book alone, you are not alone in the world! It is likely that other people have encountered similar problems to you, and that some of them will have written about their experiences.

If you browse along the autobiography/biography shelves at a bookshop or library you will see how different people have worked through grief, divorce, disablement, illness and almost any other problem you can think of. The following are just a few examples.

Family Values by Phyllis Burke (Abacus, 1993). An account of a lesbian mother's fight for her son.
Now and Then by Roy Castle (Robson Books, 1994). The last section of the book is a moving account of his fight with, and death from, cancer.
Freddie by Sarah Key (Mandarin, 1991). A diary of a cot death.
Family by Susan Hill (Penguin, 1990). An account of the death of a baby and the author's struggle to produce a second child.
No Cake No Jam by Marian Hughes (Mandarin, 1994). A stirring account of surviving hardship in childhood.
Tim: An Ordinary Boy by Colin and Wendy Parry (Coronet, 1994). Tim was killed by an IRA bomb when he was fourteen. This is an affecting account of his parents' journey through their despair.
Grey Is the Colour of Hope by Irina Ratushinskaya (Sceptre, 1988). An inspiring book by the Russian poet who was imprisoned.

These people's experiences can never be exactly the same as yours; reading about them will not solve your problems, but it can be enormously reassuring and helpful to know that others have suffered and survived. Knowing how they faced their challenges will encourage you to challenge your belief that you can never look forward to future happiness.

If you are not attracted by the idea of reading, you can talk to people. You may know someone who has come through similar problems to those which you are facing now. Make a point of talking to them; ask them how they managed; share your own fears and worries. Most people are only too pleased to talk about their own experience and want to be helpful.

EXERCISE

When reviewing your situation ask yourself these questions.

- Do I know anyone who has gone through similar experiences and managed them in the way I would like?
- Is there a book, film or play which could shed light on my situation?
- Is there an organisation which exists to advise or support people with my kind of problems?

Consequences of loss

There are many ways in which information can contribute new light on a situation, so it may prove fruitful for you to challenge yourself at this stage by seeking out any available information on your situation. You need to ask yourself something like, 'Where could I possibly find someone or something who knows more than I do about this?' For instance, a great deal has been written about the psychological and social changes which surround particular problem situations. Bereavement is a good example. When we lose someone we love, it can feel as if our world has ended – as if there is no point in living. The early days of bereavement are very painful, and we can be assailed by a range of intense feelings which are hard to contain. A great fear that people have at a time like this is that the pain will last forever and even turn into madness. We know, though, through the work of writers like Elizabeth Kubler-Ross and Colin Murray Parkes, that when we are grieving we go through more or less predictable stages and that each stage has a healing function. The following are the major features of reaction to bereavement:

- A process of acceptance following denial or avoidance of the reality of the situation.
- A period of anxiety and restlessness; feelings of fear and alarm.
- A strong urge to seek and find the lost person.
- Intense feelings of anger and guilt, perhaps directed towards those who try to help the bereaved person come to terms with the loss too quickly.
- Deep feelings of loss of self, sometimes followed by the adoption of the habits, mannerisms or symptoms of the lost person.

Knowing this does not make the situation less painful, of course, but it does help to make sense of what is happening. It can be very distressing to find oneself, or someone to whom one is close, acting irrationally or self-destructively. However, each stage of the grieving process has a healing function – this is the way we come to terms with what has happened. It is the view of practitioners who specialise in bereavement counselling that, although painful, this process is a healthy one which should not be impeded. Because there is no definite timescale for these stages, it is very easy for the process to be blocked. We might sense that other people are embarrassed by displays of grief, for instance. Or we discover that we can guard against intensely painful feelings by frenetic activity. Thinking back to Chapter 5, you can see how failure to complete the natural bereavement process becomes another piece of 'unfinished business'.

It is interesting also to realise that this process, described so far as the effect of the loss of a loved person, seems to come into play when we are facing any serious loss in our life, such as the loss of a job, health or home.

The effects of loss are felt in our mind, body and spirit. Physical symptoms which accompany the grieving process can include loss of appetite, insomnia, digestive upsets, palpitations, headaches and muscle aches and pains. The way we think is also affected; we can feel confused, lack concentration, become forgetful or lose touch with reality. Feelings of irrational anger and guilt can overcome us. A pang of grief is felt as acute anxiety and pain of the spirit. All of these reactions are natural, but if they are not understood they can feel abnormal.

EXERCISE

As you look back over the details of your situation and your analysis of what is happening, check for any evidence that you are still reacting to some important loss in your life. This may be the case if you become aware of a pattern of chronic physical symptoms, such as panic attacks, digestive upsets and headaches, which seem to have no particular trigger. Can you detect any repetitious patterns of thinking or feeling for which there seems to be no obvious explanation? Perhaps you are sometimes overcome with feelings of sadness or anger which have no apparent cause. Or you may find yourself yearning for something or someone many years after their loss. If so, consider the possibility that you are still reacting to some important loss in your life – it may be a long time ago, and it may be of a person or of an important element of your life.

If you are able to link your present symptoms with some loss in the past, consider how you might come to terms with what has happened. Gestalt exercises (see Chapter 5) are often very helpful, allowing you to give voice to thoughts and feelings which may be blocking your freedom to move forward in your life.

Reflection

You may be wondering why at this point I am suggesting spending so much time trying to find a new way of thinking about your situation. Having a problem can be exhausting. Maybe you think about it constantly with painful feelings, or you may use up a lot of energy avoiding thinking and feeling; either way you end up tired and jaded. Creating a solution, though, needs energy, and that energy will come with the excitement of realising that you can think, feel and behave differently. As you begin to change, even in small ways, you will be taking more control of your life. Finishing the work of this chapter means that you have prepared the ground for taking the action needed for the changes you want to make. But before taking that step you are due for a break. Turn to Chapter 7 to find out how.

7

Take a Break

Take rest; a field that has rested gives a
bountiful crop.

Ovid, 43 BC – AD 18

By now you can see that counselling is a logical process.
First you decided what you wanted to change and made a
contract; then you explored your situation in several ways.
You told your story and then searched the past for clues to
help you understand how you had got to this point in your
life. You then focused on what you were thinking, feeling
and doing 'here and now', so that you could begin to see
what might be changed.

You are poised for the next step, which is an important
one because it will lead you to action. All the thinking and
feeling you have experienced through the work so far has
been valuable. Some may have been painful or confusing;
some enlightening and therapeutic. However, in itself it
might not be sufficient to create the 'new you'.

As at every stage of the process, you may feel that you
have done enough. The change you were hoping for may
have come about as a result of the work so far, or you may
decide that you don't want to change anything after all.
However, if that hasn't happened yet it looks as if there is
more to do.

But not just yet! To have worked through the book so far
is a big achievement and you deserve a break. Counsellors

play many roles; listening, reflecting, challenging, questioning, focusing and making connections are all ways in which they try to help you. They also aim to provide a caring climate where you can build up your self-esteem and strength. They will be on the look-out for ways in which you under-value yourself or your abilities, encouraging you to be proud of what you have achieved so far. It is well known that children achieve better in an atmosphere where they are valued, and there is no reason to believe that as grown-ups we are any different.

So this chapter is about giving yourself a little time to relax and gather your strength for the next task. We have two targets. The first is to check that you are looking after yourself well enough – your mind, body and spirit are your chief resources, so it is important that they are in as good a state as possible. The second is to give yourself a reward for the effort you have made so far.

Set aside a specific length of time for this stage. You might decide to use one session or maybe more. Keep to the time you decide and review the situation at the end. If you would like to devote more time, again set a specific length of time.

Firstly, we will aim at target one – how well are you looking after yourself? In this section we will consider some of the main elements which contribute to your wellbeing.

Boast about it!

Our state of mind has a great effect on our health; self-esteem is an important factor in our general health and outlook on life. Small children tend to delight in their achievements. In our early years we are egocentric – we don't really understand the effect we have on others, so it seems reasonable to us that we should talk about ourselves all the time. But it is not long before most of us get a very strong 'Don't boast about yourself' message. It is true that society would be pretty terrible if everyone only talked about themselves and their achievements, but what we seem to do is decide that we should *never* let ourselves be pleased and proud. This exercise is a chance to redress the balance. It is a good one to do in a group where everyone can share their experience at the end. If you are working alone, be especially careful not to let your 'censor' take over by discounting the items you think of.

EXERCISE

Take at least ten minutes to survey your life from your earliest childhood memory onwards. Remember each achievement, each award, every single thing you accomplished. Learning to walk and talk were probably the first major achievements – don't forget to include them.

Watch out for your 'censor' and eliminate any undercutting remarks like 'I learned to swim by the time I was five. That was only because we lived by the sea and I had plenty of opportunity to practise.' 'I got my driving licence first time. But it was probably because the examiner was very generous.' In each case the first sentence is good and the second is unnecessary.

Make a point of including any events where your participation made a difference, where the outcome was influenced by your actions. For instance, 'I helped my sister learn to read'; 'I was able to comfort my Mum when my Dad died.'

Think also about times when you did something that might be easy for other people but difficult for you. 'I climbed up a tree to rescue a cat even though I'm afraid of heights'; 'I'm not usually assertive, but I told my boss that I thought he was being unfair.'

If you are doing the exercise alone, write out a brief description of each of the sections. Leave the lists for a while and then reread them. Check to see if you have let some discounts slip in – discounting means unwittingly ignoring information relevant to the solution of a problem, and you can read more about it below. If you have allowed any discounts to creep in, take them out and let yourself be truly proud of yourself. All these achievements, whether big or small, contribute to the resources you can bring to the changes you will soon be making. Remember that your level of self-esteem will affect how you think and feel. In order to get the most out of life, you need to have a realistic measure of your self-esteem – not too high, but definitely not too low!

More about discounts

If the concept of discounts is new to you, the next section will be of particular interest. The way we can discount ourselves was something that concerned some of the therapists who developed Transactional Analysis. They saw that we only had two options every time we meet a problem. One is to use our ability to think, feel and act rationally to solve the problem, and the other is to go into the script behaviour which we explored in Chapter 4. Moving into script means seeing the world so that it fits the decisions you made as an infant and closing your awareness of some aspects of the real situation. At the same time you can enlarge other aspects of the actual problem so that they take on huge proportions.

Imagine that you are in a shop wanting to buy something. You are waiting at the counter but the assistant doesn't take any notice of you. You might start feeling depressed and hopeless – or perhaps you get angry and make loud complaining comments like, 'Isn't there anyone giving service around here!' Each of these responses could be replays of very early situations. The first might stem from a time in infancy when you had wanted Mother or Father but they hadn't come. You might have believed at that time that it didn't matter how much you tried – they would never come. The second response might also arise from a script decision – that people would never recognise your importance and the only way to be heard was to shout.

The point about both responses is that neither solves the problem! Each ignores the present reality which includes options like asking the assistant for attention, going to another counter, leaving the shop, using the waiting time to relax, talking to other people in the queue and so on. Discounts can seriously affect how you manage life's problems, so it is useful to identify any ways in which you might be overlooking reality.

In any situation there are three areas of possible discount: yourself, others and the situation. Within these areas there are varying levels of depth. Let's take as an example the parents of a teenager who insists on smoking. They can discount:

- that the problem actually *exists* (parents don't notice)
- that the problem is *significant* (parents notice but tell themselves that their son is not smoking very much – and anyway it's better than taking drugs or drinking too much)
- that things could *change* (the parents are concerned about how much their son is smoking, but believe that there is no way they can stop it happening)
- *personal power* (the parents notice, they are concerned, they feel they can't do anything but hope that the teachers at school will have more influence)

This example looks at how the parents are discounting themselves at the four possible levels. They could also be discounting their child, as well as the situation.

You can usually tell when you (or someone else) is discounting some aspect of reality by noticing behaviour which can often be linked to discounting:

- *Doing nothing* (parents say nothing; teenager continues smoking)
- *Over-adapting*, which means being more concerned about what people will think of you than about anything else (parents say nothing because they are afraid their child will stop liking them; teenager smokes because 'everyone else does')
- *Agitation*, which involves purposeless, non goal-oriented activity like pacing up and down, foot-jiggling, gestures, incessant talking and so on (parents argue a lot between themselves; teenager bangs about the house)
- *Incapacitation/violence*, which might include getting ill, attacking someone, having a breakdown and so on. It might seem a bit over-dramatic to include these as categories of behaviour stemming from discounts, but they are the logical conclusion of escalating agitation. They involve an inexorable refusal to think and solve problems. They act out the belief that there is no other solution (parents hit teenager; teenager hits back, leading to breakdown of relationship; smoking continues)

EXERCISE

Use this idea to review a problem situation which you did not solve at the time. Note down whether you were discounting any aspects of the situation from the point of view of yourself, any others involved and the situation itself. Also note which of the four levels were being discounted.

Did you respond by doing nothing, over-adapting, agitation, incapacitation or violence?

Can you think of any ways in which you could have acted more satisfactorily?

Take charge of your thoughts

Exploring how you may be discounting yourself is another way of trying to understand how the way you think affects your behaviour. This ability to control how we think is one of the keys to counselling. Meditation offers methods to help you to take charge of your thoughts and create a centre of calmness within yourself. More and more people are turning towards meditation as a way of reducing stress; it is a tool which you can use to very good effect to help you in difficult times.

There are many different techniques, and no particular one is really any better than the rest. You can experiment with different ways until you find one which suits you. Here are some examples:

EXERCISE

Find a place in which you can be comfortable and uninterrupted. There is no need to adopt a special position unless you are following a particular school of meditation. Sit in a chair which gives you good support, or sit on the floor if you are more comfortable there.

Breathe slowly and deeply, relax the muscles of your face and jaw and close your eyes. When you are breathing rhythmically, count as you breathe in, pause and then allow the same count for the out-breath. Your breathing should be gentle and quiet.

It is best to meditate once a day at a regular time; early in the morning is ideal. Start by giving yourself fifteen minutes – you will soon sense whether you want to increase or decrease the time. You can develop your meditation in the following ways:

Focus on an object

Choose an object which has some positive meaning for you. It could be a candle, a vase, a rock, a tree, a flower, a picture or anything else. Use the structure above to settle yourself and then concentrate all your attention on the object. Look at it as if you had never seen it before. Close your eyes and see it in your mind; then open your eyes and re-focus. You will probably find your attention wandering; if so notice what you were thinking about and then bring your thoughts back to your object. 'Now I've started thinking about what I should make for dinner tonight. I'll let that go for now and get back to my vase/candle/tree or whatever.'

Focus on breathing

You can use your counting as the focus for your meditation, just counting each breath; forwards on the in-breath and backwards on the out-breath. 'Breathing in 1 – 2 – 3 – 4 – 5 – 6; holding 1 – 2 – 3; breathing out 6 – 5 – 4 – 3 – 2 – 1; holding 3 – 2 – 1.' Once again, if you find yourself thinking of anything other than your counting, gently bring yourself back to the task.

Focus on thoughts

This is a particularly good meditation for anyone wanting to increase their awareness of the 'here and now'. You focus on just what is happening from second to second. Each time you notice something give it a label in your mind. 'I can hear birdsong; raindrops; a clock ticking; an ambulance passing outside' and so on. Also note any physical sensation of which you become aware: 'I can feel my left foot twitching/my head feels heavy/my back is tense.' Label any thoughts that come into your head: 'I'm thinking about the shopping/the meeting/John/the argument this morning.' You may find yourself replaying some memory which is painful – if you do, notice that and give it a label: 'I'm feeling sad again/I'm remembering how angry I was.' It is the act of consciously labelling these thoughts and feelings that allows you to become more of an observer of your thinking process than reacting to it.

Focus on a word

Another possibility is that you choose a word or phrase that has some significance for you: 'Peace'; 'Love'; 'I am calm'; 'I can change' or whatever. You can chant your phrase out loud, whisper it or think it to yourself. Create a rhythm and stay with it. As before, if you distract yourself, notice, label and return to the task in hand.

Any of these methods will help you clear your mind and adopt the role of dispassionate observer of yourself which is so useful. Other benefits of regular meditation can be less reaction to stress, lowered heartbeat, lowered blood pressure, slower respiration, relief of headaches and muscle tension.

Give your body a chance

Up to now we have given a lot of attention to your mind, because counselling is, in the main, a cerebral activity. Even when you are experiencing or remembering intense feelings, you have to use your mind to think and communicate. But don't forget you have a body too! Mind and body are all part of the same system; mind and emotions are affected by the health of your body. In the same way that we can look to the past for reasons for the way in which we express some of our personality, the past is also influential on the health we have now. Leaving aside our genetic inheritance and environmental dangers that we can't control, there's still a lot for which we can take responsibility. Breathing, eating and exercise are all under our control, and all have an important part to play in our general health.

Take a breath

Breathing is essential to life; we do it all the time but we don't pay a great deal of attention to it. You will have noticed that breathing is the key to meditation – in fact good breathing plays an important part in our general health, particularly in creating a relaxed state to counteract stress. Here are two exercises which will help you assess how well you are breathing now and how to change if you need to.

EXERCISE

Without doing anything different, just notice how you are breathing at the moment.

- How do you breathe in? Through your nose, mouth or both?
- How do you breathe out?
- How far down your body is your breath reaching?
- When you breathe, do any parts of your body move?
- How many breaths per minute?
- When you breathe out, is all the air exhaled?
- Now lie on your back, with your knees pointing to the ceiling and your feet flat on the floor.

Breathe in gently through your nose, let your abdomen rise at the beginning of the breath and then your chest, and finally your shoulders can slightly lift.

When you feel it is time to breathe out, open your mouth slightly and breathe out on the sound 's-s-s-s-s-'. When the breath feels finished, squeeze out just a little more air and, when you have no more breath, let go and fill your lungs.

This exercise demonstrates the importance of breathing

out. Check whether you have got into the habit of not breathing out as much of the used air as possible to make room for a fresh intake. Our body can survive on half-lung-fuls of air – but the residue of toxins and stale air left in our lungs eventually takes its toll. The following method of breathing ensures that you fill and empty your lungs efficiently:

EXERCISE

Stand or sit. Before you begin, think of your spine as a straight line. Let your shoulders drop, feel your head balanced lightly on your neck, slightly pull in your chin and pull up the back of your head so that your spine straightens. It might help you to imagine that, like a puppet, you have a string attached to the top of your head and that the puppeteer is gently pulling it upwards. Your forehead should still point forward.

- Breathing through your nose, push out your abdomen and fill the lower part of your lungs first.
- Then let the middle part of your lungs fill, pushing out your lower ribs and sternum (breastbone).
- Lastly, fill the upper part of your lungs, letting your shoulders lift slightly.
- Hold the breath for a moment or two and then exhale slowly, drawing in your abdomen as you do so.

You might need to practise this breathing before it becomes easy, but it is worth persisting. This kind of deep, rhythmic breathing is an excellent way of coping with anxiety because it will help you regain your body–mind balance.

Eat, drink and be healthy

The population seems to be divided into two types. There are those who are preoccupied with food – what is good for you, what is bad, how much to eat, when to eat and so on; and those who never think about it and eat anything they fancy whenever they like.

Like everything we are aiming for, balance is what is required. Your body has a marvellous capacity for converting what you eat and drink into energy to power the various systems that keep you alive, so it makes sense to put in the very best. There are many theories about what composes the healthiest diet and I am not going to add to the complications. Most experts agree that some of the everyday 'props' we can get to depend on are bad for our health in the long run – these include caffeine, tranquillisers, alcohol, junk fast-food and sugar. The most sensible thing is to choose a diet which follows general health guidelines and which suits you. But don't follow it so slavishly that it becomes a punishment – the occasional bar of chocolate, slice of white bread or cup of coffee is not going to do you major harm. Just aim for a balance of protein, carbohydrate, fats and vitamins, make sure you eat some fresh vegetables and fruit every day, and avoid too much fat and sugar.

EXERCISE

Keep a note of what you eat and drink over two or three days. Don't leave anything out – even the smallest snack. Consider the list and assess its health potential. Begin to make changes if you realise that you are not eating as wisely as you could.

If over-eating is a problem for you, try this Gestalt exercise.

EXERCISE

Conjure up an image in your mind to represent your Over-eater. Take time to look at it (or him or her) and describe how you feel about its food binges.

In your mind's eye, change places and be your Over-eater and justify your behaviour. Tell yourself why you need to eat and what eating does for you. Does the food symbolise emotional nourishment of any kind? Explain what conditions would have to be necessary for you to stop.

Now change places again. Take a pause and notice if you understand any more about the Over-eater in you. For instance, do you have any ideas how the nourishment the Over-eater craves could be provided differently?

Keep moving

The link between regular exercise and mind/body fitness is not new. For instance, the ancient Chinese practice of Tai Chi and the Indian discipline of Yoga are accepted as having beneficial physical and mental effects and are practised by many people in the West. However, in modern times the link between exercise and mental health has been the subject of much research. This research has resulted, for instance, in the use of aerobic exercise to slow down decline of mental processes due to aging as well as rehabilitation from a range of psychological disorders. In 1984, for instance, Mcann and Holmes showed that when depressed women took part in an aerobic exercise class they showed greater reduction in depression than did those who either just did relaxation exercises or had no treatment.

How long is it since you set out to do some sustained exercise? This morning? Last week? Last year? Can't remember?

The programme you set yourself will depend on your

present level of fitness and your preferences. If you like company, there are aerobic, dance, keep-fit and movement groups in every part of the country. Tennis, squash, golf, bowls, cricket and football are all games which provide the pleasure of friendly competition and valuable exercise.

If the very idea of joining in physical exercise with others turns you off you can benefit from walking, running or swimming on your own, provided you set aside regular times – say half an hour three times a week. But before starting any exercise programme, it is wise to check with your general practitioner first.

Muscle relaxation is an important benefit of exercise. You know how tense you can become when you are under stress. After exercise, muscles are relaxed and calm. Exercise can also help clear the mind: it's amazing how going for a walk, run or swim can really help you sort out a difficult problem.

Target one has been to give some attention to yourself – how you think, how you rest, how you exercise and how you eat. Your mind and body are far more valuable than any piece of machinery you will ever own. If you have a car which falls to pieces you can replace it with a new one or do without. The same cannot be said of your mind and body! So it seems reasonable to give it at least the same attention you would to a valuable piece of machinery.

Treat your spirit

Target two is giving yourself a reward for getting this far. You have given your mind and body a lot of attention; now it's time to attend to your spirit, to give yourself a treat. How you do this depends entirely on your wishes and resources. Here are some suggestions:

- Take a long, scented, bubbly bath
- Have a manicure/pedicure/hairdo

- Have a massage
- Read a book/watch a video
- Take a picnic to the local park
- Phone a friend
- Paint a picture/write a poem
- Buy yourself a bunch of flowers
- Look through old photo albums
- Play a favourite tape/record
- Your own suggestions....

If you have no problem with this idea, miss the next bit and just get on with enjoying yourself. But if you are wondering why this invitation to frivolity is in the book at all, read on.

In the 1950s, a psychologist called Skinner wrote about how the principles which related to how people learn could be related to everyday life. One of these principles is that people tend to repeat behaviours for which they are in some way rewarded. What makes an effective reward?

Value

The most effective rewards are those which are highly valued by the individual. That is why it is important that you decide on what reward you want to give yourself rather than just do what I or someone else suggest.

Strength

A good reward also needs to be strong enough to make a difference to you. For one person a walk in the park may be only slightly rewarding, whereas for someone else it might be very fulfilling.

Benefit

Link the reward to behaviour that will benefit you in the

long run. Because we are so motivated by reward, undesirable behaviour will persist if rewarded. Take, for example, a child whose parents pay it attention only when it throws a tantrum, and then wonder why the child keeps throwing tantrums!

Better from you than anyone else

In the long run, the rewards which you experience for being the way you want are more effective than rewards from the outside world. For example, the reward of feeling more energy and health from your exercise programme will be more powerful than encouragement from me to start and maintain it.

The sooner the better

To be its most effective a reward should come as soon as possible after the behaviour that you want to continue. Ideally, you could give yourself some reward after each counselling session; as you make progress the counselling will come to feel rewarding in itself.

Reflection

If you have noticed yourself resisting the ideas in this chapter, it would be worth reflecting on the possible origin of the resistance. Perhaps you have developed a script which makes it hard for you to treat yourself as valuable. Why not challenge that script, reread the chapter and begin to give yourself the kind of consideration you would give to your best friend!

By now I hope I've persuaded you of the importance of a little reward, so put the book down and indulge yourself. In Chapter 8 we will begin the work again.

8

Words into Deeds

Our deeds determine us, as much as we determine
our deeds.

George Eliot, 1819–80, Adam Bede

The point we have reached is a crucial one in the counselling process. You have thought, felt, analysed and, if you
are working with others, talked about your past and life as it
is now. You have identified the changes that you feel would
make things better for you. It is possible that the process of
communicating your thoughts and feelings and understanding why they are as they are has been enough for you to
have achieved your goals.

You may, though, want more. Maybe you want to try out
different behaviour, achieve more than you are at present,
make more satisfying relationships, get a better job or whatever. If so, it is time to take action. Thinking and talking do
help you to clarify matters – but it usually takes more to
effect significant change. To be successful, you will have to
take action – turn the words into deeds. This is a good time
to check over the contract for change you made in Chapter
2. The work we have done so far will have prepared the
ground for making those changes, and so it is appropriate at
this point to confirm that your contract is the best one
possible. These are questions which will help you make a
review:

EXERCISE

Look back on the contract you made in Chapter 2.
Write down your answers to these questions:

- What have I got so far from working through this book?
- What have I been doing to get what I want?
- Have I been stopping myself in any way?
- How do I feel about my contract now?
- Am I asking too much or too little of myself?
- How committed am I to continuing the process?
- Is there anything else I could be doing to maximise my chances of succeeding?

The focus of this chapter is to turn your contract into achievable goals. If your contract covers more than one area, you need to decide whether you want to work on one at a time or on two or more together. The first task is to check that you are not setting yourself up to fail by working to unrealistic expectations. Notice how you have stated your wishes. Have you, for instance, made rather general statements like 'I want to work harder to make my relationship better'; 'I want to get healthier'; 'I want to take charge of my life? These are what Gerard Egan, a psychologist who has developed a helpful counselling model which includes a structure for setting action goals, calls 'statements of intent'.

Aims and goals

Statements of intent are a good place to start, but in themselves are not detailed enough to help you decide exactly what to do. A counsellor would encourage you to be more specific, firstly by converting the statements into *aims*. An aim identifies the area in which you want to work.

Leila is talking about her relationship with her teenage son. 'I can see that I don't give him enough encouragement. I've got to be more accepting.' Then she clarifies her aims: 'It isn't that I don't love him, but I don't like the way he behaves towards me and his father. I retaliate by ignoring him, which I know makes things worse. I want to change how I respond to him – talk to him more and find out what he thinks about things.' You can see how this is not quite so vague as the original statement.

Aims tend to materialise as the problem is defined clearly. For instance, Martin is recovering from a heart attack. He went to a meeting of a self-help group set up by the hospital. He heard the other members talk about how they were facing their problems. He said, 'I realise, as I've been listening to all of you, that I've been very lazy in taking control of my recovery. I've been very depressed, and I can see that by being so passive I haven't improved as much as I might have done.' Notice how, although Martin has identified how his own response might be contributing to his problems, he hasn't yet said what he is going to do to handle things better.

On being encouraged to talk in more detail he mused, 'I used to care a lot about how I looked, and chose my clothes carefully. But since my illness I've let myself go. I used to enjoy walking, but I just haven't felt like it recently.' You can see how he is beginning to identify definite areas where he could make changes.

EXERCISE

Look over your contract again; turn any general statements you have made into a set of aims. You can do this by asking yourself, 'What could I do that would lead towards what I want.' For example, if one of your aims was to improve your health and fitness, the answer might be: 'I could take more exercise, change my diet, be more relaxed', etc.

However, you can do still more to ensure success when you begin to take action by converting your aims into goals. Goals are clear expressions of what you can actually do to handle a problem situation or some part of it. Notice how different it would be if Martin were to say, 'I'm going to have a haircut on Friday and buy a new outfit on Saturday. During the week I will take a walk round the park at least three times.' What he will actually be *doing* is much clearer; he is no longer just *thinking* about the problem.

At this stage, we are borrowing ideas from behavioural approaches – so called because they are focused on helping clients to identify and change the behaviour which may be causing problems. We are using a method which is based on carefully set goals. Goals are the practical steps which will take you towards the changes you want. By the time you have finished this chapter you will be well on the way to the next part of your journey. When helping a client set goals, a counsellor will have certain principles in mind to create a secure framework within which the client is likely to succeed. These questions will enable you to do the same.

Principles of goal setting

These are the questions to ask yourself about the goals you want to set:

What will I be able to do when I have carried out this goal?

Describe your goal by explaining what you will actually be doing when you have arrived, rather than what you are going to do to get there. For instance, a goal like 'I'll go swimming every morning' relates to the process which could lead to the aim of getting healthy, but it doesn't in itself tell you what you are aiming for. Your goal is achieved when you have reached the level of fitness you want.

Gerard Egan calls this the 'past participle' approach to goal setting – smoking *stopped*; weight *decreased*; bad temper *controlled*; new job *acquired*; and so on.

Can I see myself doing what I propose?

As you think about a possible goal, visualise yourself actually doing it. This is the best way to check that you are clear enough about what you are aiming for. 'In six months from now, I will be swimming a mile at least three times a week' is clearer than 'I'll get fitter by going swimming'. It is also important to set a reasonable time-frame for the work.

How will I know that I am making progress?

It may sound obvious to say that you ought to be able to tell whether you have achieved your goals or not, but it is important to have some kind of measure. If you don't know where you are starting a journey, how will you know if you are moving quickly enough in the right direction? If you don't know when you've arrived, how will you know when you can stop travelling? So the goals that you set should be measurable or evident. Improving a relationship, for instance, can be measured by a reduction in the number of arguments or an increase in the amount of time spent together. If when you started you were having at least three serious rows a day, and when you put your goals into action these are down to one a month, things have obviously improved. Not everything can be quantified in this way, however; another way of judging the effectiveness of a goal is to look for evidence of change.

Peter, having set goals to increase his job satisfaction, might say, 'Since I spoke to my manager about my feeling that I wasn't being mentally stretched as much as I'd like, I've been given more interesting jobs. I enjoy going to work now and feel much happier.'

Have I got what it takes?

It is better to set goals that are within your own resources than those which depend on outside circumstances. This means taking care to set goals which are realistic and within your reach. Beware of setting goals which are too high – as you try to reach them, you may constantly fall short and give up. A baby learning to walk is a good model. Most babies don't look around them one day, see everyone else walking, say to themselves, 'I want to do that', and then get up and walk! The majority of babies spend a long time getting to the stage when they can stand up on their own – and then fall down first time they try. Yet I've never seen a baby go into a fit of depression because it couldn't walk first time it tried! Most babies go on trying, falling down and getting up again until – one day – they walk unaided. Use this as your model for the changes you want to make.

Realism is at the heart of this principle. For instance, it would be unrealistic to want to leave your job and go to university if you are not entitled to a grant and don't have the money or academic grades necessary. A more realistic goal would be to continue working and take evening classes for the time being.

Another barrier which might stop you is not paying enough attention to the environment in which you are hoping to achieve change. Moving into a larger house might seem to be the answer to your problems, but if property prices are too high you would need to think again. Setting interim goals of rearranging your present home would be more sensible.

One more consideration is that undertaking the goal should be under your control. If you decide to swim three time a week but need someone to give you a lift to the nearest pool, you might find that through no fault of your own you can't carry the goal through. It would be more realistic to think of exercise which did not depend on someone else's help.

Yet another danger is to make a goal based on someone else changing their behaviour. Wendy is unhappy because her father treats her as if she is still a child. 'My goal is that he will treat me more seriously' is probably doomed to failure because she cannot guarantee that her father will do what she wants. If she sets a goal to change her own behaviour, for example 'I will think out what I want to say and rehearse it. I will ask him to let me finish what I want to say before he gives me his opinion', she is more likely to succeed. There is no way of guaranteeing that her father will listen to her or take her seriously, but by taking the initiative in saying what she wants Wendy is at the very least strengthening her communication skills. Of course she hopes for more than this, but whatever happens she can have the satisfaction of knowing that she carried through her resolve to speak up.

Is what I propose going to be enough?

We have established that goals should not be set too high, but this does not mean they should be so low that they make hardly any difference to the situation. If you have never shared household chores, offering to wash up once a month is unlikely to be enough to create a more equal relationship.

How valuable is my goal to me?

When you are setting your goals, make certain that what you propose fits into your own value system. It is so easy to fall into the trap of setting goals to please someone else. Counsellors often have to resist giving advice to clients at this stage. It might seem easier to ask someone what to do, but if it is in conflict with our own values it is unlikely that we will follow the advice – however good it is. Of course, there is a hidden advantage in this situation – if we fail we can always blame the adviser!

EXERCISE

The following structure will help you use the frame-work we have explored. It is in the form of a set of statements for you to finish, either by writing or speaking to a tape. If you are working with a partner or a group, take it in turns to go through the structure, helping each other to keep within the principles described above.

- My overall intention is:
- Aims that would lead to that are:
- The aim I will work on first is:
- Goals that will lead to that aim are:
- Complete the next set of statements for each goal:
- When I have finished the goal I will have:
- I will be able to measure my success by:
- Evidence of my success will be:
- I will need the following resources:
- What I propose to do is realistic because:
- It is adequate because:
- It is valuable to me because:
- I will begin on:
- I will review the situation on:

Why bother?

This stage can be seen as the midway point in your journey. Everything up to this point has been in preparation for making changes. Everything after this point will be to support the achievement of the goals you set. You may be tempted to skip over this careful goal setting, especially if you have a lot of ideas about the changes you want to make. However, your long-term success depends a great deal on how you manage this process. One of the main reasons that people fail to maintain changes is that they move too quickly into action without taking time to consider all the implications.

Derek, for instance, was very lonely and found it difficult to make relationships with the opposite sex. Yet he very much wanted to get married and have a family. He had never had an intimate partner and felt that time was passing him by. As he thought about his early life, an only child of parents who were in constant conflict, it became apparent that he had developed a script which would protect him from the violence and unhappiness he experienced as a child: 'If I don't start a relationship, I can't be hurt.'

Once he realised that he might be unnecessarily holding back, he decided to branch out. He started attending singles clubs, placed advertisements in a 'seeking partners' column, and dated women from his office.

But things didn't go as well as he hoped. He felt awkward in the company of women, not knowing what to say or do to create the atmosphere he wanted. He was either too diffident or too aggressive, and found that no one seemed interested in making more than one date with him.

He realised that he had launched into action without thinking out his goals carefully. There were several areas in which he could set goals to prepare the ground – for instance meeting more women, becoming more self-confident, learning how to manage social situations and so on. Concluding that he needed to improve his social and communication skills in more supportive surroundings, he joined a course on interpersonal communication skills offered by his local adult education centre.

It's easy to make the same mistake as Derek and jump straight into action. The value of setting goals in the way we have just considered is that you can move slowly, staying in control of your progress.

Deciding how to do it

Having decided on your goals, the next step is to think about how you will carry them out. You give yourself an advantage if you can think up a variety of options. The more possibilities you have, the greater the chances of success. The problem with having only one plan is that if it doesn't work you have to go back to the beginning again. With more than one, you can just move on to the next suggestion.

Let's return to Derek. The course he attended did a great deal to increase his communication and social skills. He was able to practise through role-playing and group exercises; he found the tutor and the rest of the group very sympathetic and supportive, and his confidence grew. He thought again about his wish to meet more women and felt he was better prepared this time.

Derek thought up quite a few ways in which he could go about it. He used a very simple technique called *brainstorming*, a technique often used in the business world for generating creative ideas. You can do it on your own as a personal exercise, although it works very well when you get together with others. They don't need to know very much about your particular problem and certainly don't have to be experts. In fact it can be a boon if you do this with people who don't know you or your problem. That way you are likely to get far more creative results.

The process is very simple – but it is important to keep to the rules:

1. Explain what you want

If you are working with someone else, explain as simply as possible what you are trying to achieve, for instance 'I'm aiming to lose a stone in weight by the end of the winter'; 'I want to have changed my job by the end of the year.'

2. Explain the rules

You need as many ideas as possible on how you could carry out your goals. Tell people to come up with any ideas they have – nothing will be discussed at this point. Encourage everyone to let themselves go; any idea, however fanciful, is acceptable. Write down every suggestion, even the wildest.

3. Consider the possibilities

When everyone has run out of steam, go through the list. Mark each item with a 'yes' for those which you feel you could do and a 'no' for any which you would not consider under any circumstances. There are bound to be some items about which you cannot be absolutely certain – perhaps something which as it stands you would not consider, but with the germ of an idea which could be developed. These items should be marked 'M' for 'maybe' and could be the most important of all.

Sorting the results of brainstorming

Derek organised a brainstorming session with the other members of the course he was attending. He told them that he wanted to meet and make friends with more women. They came up with these suggestions, which Derek marked with Y, N or M for yes, no or maybe.

- Join a singles club   N
- Go to discos   N
- Pick a girl you fancy   N
- Have a party and invite your friends to bring more friends   M
- Organise an office outing   M
- Ask a friend to arrange a blind date   N
- Join a computer dating organisation   Y
- Put an ad in the local paper   M

- Answer 'lonely hearts' ads   Y
- Join the local church   Y
- Take evening classes   M
- Join a local political party   N
- Take a singles holiday   M
- Do voluntary work   Y

If you have been trying to solve a problem for some time and failing miserably, you may have come to believe that it is indeed insoluble. Once you believe that, your ability to produce creative thinking about it is likely to desert you. That is why the brainstorming idea is so useful. You give yourself permission to generate a range of ideas without having to judge whether they are sensible or not.

EXERCISE

Once you have set your goals, take the one you want to start with and organise a brainstorming session. If you are working on your own but feel you have exhausted all the possibilities you can think of, you could involve other people. Without revealing any details that you don't want to, just tell people briefly what you want them to think about. 'Supposing someone wanted to.... What do you think they could do?' 'What would you do if....' 'I'm thinking of.... How could I do it?' are possible ways of introducing the subject. Don't comment on the suggestions that people make, but note them down so that you can think about them later.

Changing behaviour

Some behaviour is very resistant to all our efforts to change. These are areas for which it is hard to find any rational explanation. Say, for instance, that you have a very high level of anxiety about taking examinations. If you haven't worked hard enough during termtime or done enough revision, it is possible to understand the root of the anxiety – and do something about it! However, for behaviour which seems to have no rational explanation one particular method has proved very useful. This approach, called systematic desensitisation, is a method used by practitioners of behavioural counselling. Three elements are involved: deep relaxation, establishing a progressive ladder of anxiety and using visualisation of each item on that ladder.

Deep relaxation

Chapter 7 describes breathing and meditation exercises, which can create a relaxed state. If you want to use relaxation as part of your action programme and have had no training, put aside some time now to work through the next exercise. It takes you through a detailed relaxation process which is based on a focus-tense-hold-release-relax cycle for each group of muscles.

EXERCISE

You will need at least twenty minutes for this exercise in a quiet room where you will be uninterrupted. You will feel more comfortable if you wear loose-fitting clothing. Tape the instructions or get someone to read them through slowly while you are learning the sequence.

Lie on your back on a firm surface, and spend a couple of minutes concentrating on your breathing.

Now focus your attention on your right hand and forearm; clench your fist and tense the muscles in your lower arm. Hold the tension for a moment, then release as quickly as you can. Let the tension go

---

further and further and allow those muscles to become more and more relaxed. Wait for one minute, then move your focus of attention to your upper right arm.

Bend the arm at the elbow and flex your biceps by tensing the muscles of your upper right arm. Hold – then release; let the tension go even further and wait for one minute.

Focus now on your left hand and forearm. Clench your left fist and tense the muscles of your forearm. Hold – then release and let the tension go further. Wait for one minute, then move the focus to your upper left arm.

Bend your left arm at the elbow and flex your biceps by tensing the muscles of your upper left arm.

Move the focus of attention now to your forehead. Lift your eyebrows as high as possible – hold – release – relax – wait.

Now focus on your eyes, nose and upper cheeks. Squeeze your eyes tightly shut and wrinkle up your nose – hold – release – relax – wait.

Attend now to your jaw and lower cheeks. Clench your teeth and pull your mouth firmly back – hold – release – relax – wait.

Now deal with your neck and throat. Pull your chin down hard towards your chest while at the same time resisting actually touching your chest – hold – release – relax – wait.

Chest and shoulders come next. Pull your shoulder blades together and take a deep breath – hold – release – relax – wait.

Stomach. Tighten the muscles in your stomach as though someone was about to hit you there – hold – release – relax – wait.

Right thigh. Tense the muscles of your right upper leg – hold – release – relax – wait.

Right calf. Stretch your right leg and pull your toes towards your head – hold – release – relax – wait.

Right foot. Point and curl the toes of your right foot and turn it inwards – hold – release – relax – wait.

Left thigh. Tense the muscles of your left upper leg – hold – release – relax – wait.

Left calf. Stretch your left leg and pull your toes towards your head – hold – release – relax – wait.

Left foot. Point and curl the toes of your left foot and turn it inwards – hold – release – relax – wait.

It is important to practise the relaxation sequence until it is second nature to you. When you have got to that stage, you can also learn brief procedures which will stand you in good stead in everyday life when you need to relax quickly. The idea is to attain a deep level of relaxation with less time and effort.

One variation is to tense larger groups of muscles in order as follows:

Group 1 right arm, left arm and face
Group 2 neck and throat
Group 3 chest and shoulders
Group 4 stomach
Group 5 left leg and foot
Group 6 right leg and foot

Simultaneous muscle relaxation involves tensing all the muscles at once, holding, releasing and relaxing as before.

Once you have mastered the skills of muscle relaxation you can move on to the second stage – creating a ladder of anxiety which is ranked according to the level of anxiety experienced in thinking about different situations. Taking examination anxiety again as an example, the ladder might look like this:

1. Thinking about exams while revising three months beforehand
2. Thinking about exams while revising two months beforehand
3. Thinking about exams while revising one month beforehand
4. Thinking about exams while revising one week beforehand
5. Thinking about exams while revising one day beforehand
6. Waking up on the morning of the exam
7. On the bus going to take the exam
8. Walking into the exam room
9. Turning over the exam paper
10. Seeing other people writing their answers
11. Having a panic attack in the exam room

EXERCISE

If there are any themes in your life which are appropriate, construct a ladder of anxiety with rung number 1 being the situation which you feel least anxious thinking about.

When we think of something which in some way threatens us, our muscles naturally tense as our bodies move into the fight/flight response to stress. The principle of this method is training your muscles to relax rather than tense up at such times. That is why learning to relax at will is so important. The idea is to take the item which causes least anxiety first, conjure up the image of yourself in that situation and then consciously relax your muscles. When you get to the stage of not feeling any anxiety at all, you can move on to the next item. In this way you are gradually training yourself in a new habit of response. If you find that you get stuck on a particular rung of the ladder, think of a less anxiety-evoking scene.

More ways of changing behaviour

Before we leave this stage, it is worth considering some other elements of the behavioural approach which you may find constructive:

Find a model

Watching someone do something that you don't know how to do, or are afraid of, can be a great way of getting started.

Rehearse

You can practise new behaviour by rehearsing what you want to say or do. You might use a tape or video recorder, or another person to help you.

Be assertive

The ability to be assertive – that is, the ability to communicate your thoughts and feelings clearly and appropriately – is one of the greatest assets in taking control of your life. Assertiveness is something you can learn – there are courses you can attend and books you can read.

Reinforcement

Research has shown that we do respond to reinforcement: we repeat behaviour which is rewarded. Behavioural counsellors often use a systematic system of reinforcement to initiate or strengthen appropriate behaviour and to weaken or eliminate inappropriate behaviour. Chapter 7 made this point by encouraging you to stop and give yourself a treat for having got so far. You can do this whenever you succeed in making a change.

The next step

At this crucial stage, one of the most important things a counsellor can do is help you retain the level of self-awareness and logical thought you may have developed during the counselling sessions. Actually beginning to make the changes you want can be quite scary. After all, you don't really know what will happen as a result and it is easy to return to the old patterns of thought, feeling and behaviour. Although they don't solve the problems, at least they are familiar – so it can feel tempting to put off the change for just a little while longer. One way of helping yourself to avoid this trap is to design a structure which will support you when you begin to make the changes.

Make a checklist of questions to ask yourself before, during and after the action. The questions are to guide you along the way and are intended as prompts so that you can avoid getting confused and losing the point of what you are trying to do, particularly if things don't go according to plan.

It is important that you identify your particular weak spots so that your list can act as a prompt. Here are some general questions that you might find useful:

Before

- What is the worst thing that can happen? Am I prepared for that?
- What are the options open to me?
- What are my expectations? Are they reasonable?
- Is there anything that is likely to add to my stress?

During

- What am I thinking and feeling?
- What am I doing?
- Do I want to continue?

- Am I listening to the others? What are they actually saying? What are they doing?
- Am I giving myself time to make a decision?

After

- How did things go?
- How far did I satisfy my expectations?
- What am I pleased with?
- Is there anything I would change?
- What is my next step?

What if it doesn't work?

Counselling doesn't automatically guarantee success. Counsellors aim to help you understand yourself and your situation so that you can identify the possible causes of problems and make the changes which would help you. They may also support you while you are taking whatever action you have decided upon – but they cannot do it for you. It's possible that, even if you do everything according to the methods we have explored, things won't go your way. If this happens to you, don't give up! You need to understand why things are going wrong.

First, give yourself a break. Taking the risk of trying to take more control of your life is in itself an achievement so take time to acknowledge this. Then check on these points:

1. Do you have a contingency plan? If you have, put it into practice now. If not, move on to the next step:
2. Go back to your original contract. Have you missed some vital step on the way to making your goals? The pattern we have been following starts with understanding what may have led up to the present problem; then exploring how you are responding now; finding a new way of seeing things; and finally

deciding on the plan of action. Maybe one of the stages has not been sufficiently explored.

3. Check that you have not lost sight of the wood for the trees. It is possible that you have got so involved in making an elaborate plan that your original intention has got swamped in the details.

4. Is what has happened in any way familiar? Sometimes we unconsciously repeat patterns of behaviour so that we replay our script once more. If you have fallen into a familiar trap, look again at the chapter about life scripts.

Reflection

This has been the phase when you committed yourself to action, and it may have been the most difficult phase of all. To have got this far on your own is an accomplishment. You probably have enough evidence by now to judge whether self-counselling is going to work for you. If it has gone successfully you will be well on the way to the kind of life you want for yourself. If not, you will be considering your next step. In Chapter 9 you will have the opportunity to review your situation in order to decide what to do next. Above all, don't lose hope. Remember how the baby learns to walk – step by step, with a great deal of falling down in between.

9

Reviewing the Situation

When you know a thing, to hold that you know it;
and when you do not know a thing, to allow that you
do not know it; this is knowledge.

Confucius, 551–478 BC

At its simplest, the main point of counselling – and of this book – is to help you take more control of your life so that you can live in a more satisfying, resourceful and happy way. We have explored some of the ways that you can use different counselling techniques to help you make the changes you want, and you are now at the point when you have been putting some of those changes into action. You might be behaving differently, thinking more clearly or using your newly raised consciousness to make decisions. Whatever the nature of the changes you are making, at this stage it would be useful to review the situation. The purpose of this chapter is to give you a way of evaluating the progress you are making so that you can decide whether to continue on the same track, change direction or stop altogether.

You will find it helpful to set aside one of your sessions on a regular basis to review your progress. Taking time every now and again to consider how you are managing your life is a very good habit to get into. If you never stop to do this you could easily find yourself persisting in some course of action which isn't working particularly well instead of trying to find out what the trouble is and putting it right.

Reasons for review

Reason 1: to assess your level of success

However clear your objectives, however specific your action plan and however strongly you are committed, there will always be some factors outside your control which could result in your not getting what you want. In any case, because you are human you will sometimes make mistakes. Your aims might not be realistic, your skills not sufficiently developed, or you might even change your mind about what you want. Planning time for a review will help you to manage your feelings and decide what to do next.

If you are not succeeding as much as you hoped, don't immediately assume that you are achieving nothing. Use the following questions to help you weigh up your level of success and separate the different elements of what is happening.

EXERCISE

Answer these self-assessment questions.

- What actually is happening?
- What is not happening?
- What am I doing, thinking, feeling?
- What am I not doing, thinking, feeling?
- How is it different from what I expected?
- Is there any way in which I have sabotaged my plan?
- What is my inner voice telling me?
- Is it true?
- Has what is happening now happened before?
- Is there any way in which I could change what I am doing, thinking, feeling?
- Is there anything that others are doing that is making it difficult for me?

- How can I communicate with them?
- Do I want to continue on this course?
- Do I have any other options?
- What can I learn from what has happened?
- Do I need to set different goals?

When things start going wrong it can feel as if everything is failing. More often than not, although the level of success is not as great as you wanted you are achieving some of your goals. Marking these successes helps to build your self-esteem – it is easier to move on from a success, however small, than to start again with the feeling of failure.

Even if you are completely successful, you will find it useful to review what has happened. It is important to identify the skills and resources that you used, because they can be used for other problems you may meet in life.

Reason 2: to help you see the wood from the trees

Establishing the level of success is not the only important reason for undertaking a regular review. This particular approach to change involves breaking down your overall intention into small action goals, so that you can move logically and safely towards meeting your wishes. You can sometimes get so involved in carrying out your action goals that you lose sight of the wood for the trees. Reviewing helps you to keep everything in perspective.

Life stage perspective   For example, consider the implications of the stage of life you have reached. It is generally accepted that childhood consists of developmental stages, each building on the one before. Children learn to walk, talk, play, read, write and so on. They also learn to deal with relationships with their parents, siblings and others.

They learn how to become social beings. When they become adolescents there is even more development. The whole search for an identity and the task of separating from parents and taking on adult responsibilities can create enormous pressures. Many experts have written about the development of children and adolescents – but not quite so much attention has been given to the fact that we continue to grow and change through our adult lives.

If you look back over your life so far you will see that at each stage you were facing different tasks, trying to answer different questions. One way of understanding this is to focus on each decade of adult life. Obviously, not everyone will fall into this neat scenario and the idea is offered as a guideline rather than as a set of rules. Don't worry if you find that you are ahead or behind – the idea is that you are able to see your present stage as part of a picture rather than the picture itself.

The twenties, our time of early adulthood, may be the first time we experience 'being on our own'. Some of the tasks facing us include:

- Achieving independence from our parents and learning to fend for ourselves
- Learning about the world of employment
- Making long-term relationships; exploring commitment to marriage and family

The kind of questions which dominate this stage are:

- How can I be myself?
- What kind of life do I want?
- What do I have to do to live in the way I want?
- How am I going to earn a living?
- Whom do I want to share my life with?

The thirties is often a time of readjustment. We may have made plans for the long term about a career or a relationship which have not turned out as we expected. Life can seem much more complex than before. Perhaps the future which seemed so full of possibilities has turned out to be more restricted than we hoped. Problems which we couldn't forecast arise. The choices made earlier in our lives may need reassessment. Life tasks can include:

- Finding out what we really want from life
- Progressing in our chosen career
- Starting a family
- Maintaining long-term relationships
- Managing possible conflicts between career and other demands in life

This is a time of change for many people as they consider questions like

- What do I really want out of life?
- How can I find out about myself?

At this time some people think about going into therapy, not because they have a particular problem but because they have the sense that things could be different and are not sure how. The search for identity becomes important as the sense of time passing is felt. For many, the question of having children is high on the agenda. For women this is a crucial decision if they have a career, for they may feel they have to choose between their career and motherhood.

The forties is the time when a good number of people experience what has commonly become known as a 'mid-life crisis' – a time of acute personal discomfort. We become more aware of the limits to fulfilling our goals. We have to compare our actual achievements with our youthful dreams. Tasks at this stage comprise:

- Establishing long-term goals
- Getting recognition in one's career

- Re-examination of personal relationships
- Assessing the gap between hopes and achievements
- Acceptance of the finite nature of time

For some, this is a stressful time. Children are growing up and going away, while parents may be becoming more dependent – it can feel as though we are being pulled in opposite directions by the demands of those around us.

Some people completely change their direction, seeking a new career or relationship. Common questions at this time are:

- What has become of my life?
- When am I going to have what I really want?
- Is this going to be my last chance to succeed?

The fifties can be a time of balancing and renewal for those who successfully negotiate their way through the sometimes painful mid-life transition. For some it is an extremely good time. In a career, status and recognition may come at this stage, perhaps with promotion. On the other hand, if recognition doesn't come it can feel a hopeless time. The financial responsibility of parenthood diminishes as children leave home. The tasks confronting us at this stage include:

- Acceptance of what we have
- Preparation for retirement from work
- Reassessment of family life as children leave home

Very often, people become clearer and more confident about their values – and sometimes distressed because those values are changing as the younger generation come to the fore.

Women have a dramatic reminder of the passing of time as they experience the menopause, which for some is physically and psychologically demanding.

The sixties is when we can expect ourselves to have arrived at maturity, accepting ourselves as we are and coming to grips with what we have and haven't achieved in life. It can be a time of beginning something we have always wanted to do because it might be the last opportunity. Retirement is on the horizon for those at work. Like most stages, this can be a positive or a negative experience; for some a time of new challenges, for others a feeling of loss.

The seventies and after bring us face to face with our aging. We may have to meet the illness or death of those close to us, and must come to terms with our own mortality. Remaining healthy and mobile are major priorities; material possessions become less important.

EXERCISE

Take a moment to reflect on the life stage you have reached.

- What do you see as the main life tasks which face you now?
- How much are the problems you are facing a product of, or influenced by, your present life stage?
- Is there anything unfinished from previous life stages?

Thinking in these general terms about your stage of life may shed light on your present problems. There is a powerful mythology surrounding the expectations of different age groups. For example, young adults are supposed to be full of energy and ambition. If you happen to be twenty-five and can't get a job, it's no surprise that you may be doubly depressed! Not only are you having to manage the difficulty of getting work, but you are not fitting into expectations of what is normal for this time of life. In middle age you are supposed to be a career success, to have a happy family life and to take civic responsibilities. How are you to cope with feeling unhappy, restless or frustrated? What if your children are behaving badly or your partner has left you? You may be experiencing unusual feelings of depression or anxiety which could be linked to your having reached mid-life.

System perspective   For most of the time you have been working through this book, the spotlight has been on you. You have been considering your thoughts, feelings and behaviour; you have been setting goals for achieving your life ambitions. Unless you are living an unusually isolated life, you are in contact with others: your family, friends and work colleagues, for example.

You could see these people as making up a system of which you are a part. Systems have structure and function. Think about your body, for instance. The nervous system is structured from brain, spinal cord and nerves, and carries impulses to and from our brain. The function of this system is communication between various parts of the body and between the body and the outside world. Our heart, veins, arteries and capillaries make up a circulation system whose function is to circulate nutrition and fluids to various parts of the body and to dispose of the waste and toxic products. Organisations have systems, too. The structure of a religion has a hierarchy of religious leaders and lay members. Its function is to provide spiritual support for its followers.

Each family has a structure and a function which affect each member. Virginia Satir suggests the image of a mobile, from which the separate pieces hang suspended in balance with each other. Although each part of the mobile is separate, it is seen as a whole. If one piece moves, every other piece is affected. If it is left alone, each piece returns to the place where it is in perfect balance with the others. How you fit into your family mobile is another aspect of your situation.

Marilyn is married to Norman, who works very hard as an industrial production manager. They have three children: Sally, who is doing very well at school and has just got into university; Adam, the middle one, quiet and unobtrusive; and the youngest, Cherry, clever and cute and always cherished as 'the baby'. Suddenly the 'family mobile' gets knocked when Norman is made redundant. Norman becomes short-tempered and depressed; Sally gets anxious that she won't be able to afford to go to university; Adam becomes even more silent; Cherry is confused because the attention she has been used to is suddenly withdrawn. Marilyn tried to keep everyone's spirits up – but begins to suffer from panic attacks. She goes to the doctor, who treats her for the physical anxiety symptoms.

Marilyn could be seen as the person with a problem; after all, she is the one who has physical symptoms. However, when you look at the whole system we can see that she is only one part of it and that everyone is affected.

EXERCISE

Imagine and draw your family 'mobile'. It should include all the individual members of your family – parents, grandparents, aunts, uncles, children and everyone else who is considered to be part of the family.

- Has any part of the mobile had a knock recently? If so, how would this have affected each other part? How has it affected you?
- If you are the one who has had the knock, how has this affected each other part?

You can extend this idea to include other people who are important to you – work colleagues, close friends and so on. Seeing yourself as part of these interconnecting relationships is another way of shedding light on your circumstances.

Your present life stage and your relationship system are two suggestions for giving yourself a wider view while you are reviewing your progress.

What if it isn't working?

It is natural to feel downhearted if all the work you have done doesn't seem to be paying off. You need to manage the setback so that it doesn't stop you in your tracks. The point of this exercise is to prepare yourself for meeting disappointment if it arises.

EXERCISE

Think back to a particular disappointment in your life. It might help to write down the details.

- What were your first reactions? How did you feel? What did you think? What did you do?
- To what extent were these typical thoughts, feelings and actions in response to disappointment?
- Coolly consider each of your reactions – which ones helped you move on and which ones kept you stuck?

Here are four ways of constructively coping with disappointment:

Expressing your feelings

We live in a society which tends to encourage people to hide the strength of their feelings, but you are bound to have an emotional response. Crying, shouting, hitting a cushion, digging the garden, going for a run or playing a hard game of squash are all ways of expressing bad feelings. As long as you don't hurt anyone, it doesn't really matter how you get rid of those feelings. Keeping them inside to hide them from others, perhaps not even admitting them to yourself, will add enormously to the stress you might already be experiencing. Bad feelings don't just disappear – the tension they create lodges in the body if it is not discharged, and then finds all sorts of ways of popping up. Looking over the previous exercise, are you satisfied with how you tend to express your feelings? If not, can you think of ways in which you could do so in the future?

Share with someone

The second means of coping with disappointment is to have someone to talk to about it. The problem for many of us is that we just have one or two people from whom we expect all of our emotional support. If this is true for you, it is worth thinking about creating a wider network of support for yourself. It may not be reasonable to expect all of your needs to be satisfied by just one or two people, whether spouse or partner, immediate family member or close friend. The following exercise makes the point that support is multi-faceted and will help you identify just who is, or could be, in your personal network.

EXERCISE

Write in the names of people you know who do, or who could, provide you with these different kinds of support.

.... is always willing to listen without judging me
.... shares their thoughts and feelings with me
.... always makes me feel competent and valued
.... can be trusted to give me constructive feedback

.... is a reliable source of information

.... will challenge me so that I don't become complacent

.... can be depended upon in a crisis

.... is someone I feel close to

.... introduces me to new ideas/interests/people

.... understands the changes I am trying to make

.... is someone with whom I can laugh or cry

Does anything surprise you when you look at your network? Are there any gaps? Do you rely on one or two people for all your support? If so, are there any consequences for you or them? Does it matter? Do you want to extend it, plug gaps or make changes?

Talk to yourself

The third element in managing the disappointment of failure is how you talk to yourself in such a situation. We are back in the territory covered in Chapter 6, where we explored how the way we talk to ourselves about our inner beliefs influences the way we behave. Learning how to control what you are thinking helps you avoid the spiral of gloom which is such a classic reaction to the collapse of our hopes.

We usually respond to an unfortunate event by feeling bad, and then assume that the bad feelings are caused by the event. However, that is not the whole story. In fact, when something bad happens we respond to it by converting the experience into thoughts. These are the words we hear in our head, and they determine our feelings which in turn affect what we do.

Harriet failed her driving test. As soon as she was given the result she told herself, 'I'm pathetic. I've failed something that anyone can do. Everyone will think I'm stupid –

I'm not trying again because I'll just keep on failing.' In response she felt hopeless, ashamed, embarrassed and frustrated. If she had acted on the strength of those feelings it is likely that she would have given up altogether so as not to put herself at risk again.

All of this comes from the assumption that our feelings are caused by the things that happen to us, rather than from our interpretation of the event. You will be familiar with your own favourite self-talk habits from some of the exercises you have already done. Now would be a good time to practise substituting a more constructive response.

Harriet, for instance, could have said to herself, 'I'm disappointed because I wanted to pass this time. I know I practised hard and did my best. Now I have experience of what a test is like, I'll know what to expect next time. I know what mistakes I made, and won't make them again. I've failed the test – but that doesn't make *me* a failure.'

Looking back again to what you said you did when facing disappointment, notice what you said to yourself. If it was negative self-talk, what might you have said that could be more positive?

EXERCISE

Tick the statements to which you can answer 'yes'.

- Do I have a regular exercise programme?
- Am I following a balanced diet and eating regularly?
- Do I have a regular schedule of work and play?
- Am I giving myself a break when I need it?
- Do I reward myself for my achievements?
- Do I have people to turn to for support?
- Do I know how to relax?
- Do I know how to talk constructively to myself?

> Think carefully about any item to which you have to answer 'no'. What would you have to do to turn this into a 'yes'?

Getting support

You may decide that working through this book on your own, or with others, is not working sufficiently to help you with all the situations you want to change.

Many people find themselves without the kind of natural support which seemed to exist more in the past. Years ago, for example, people could depend on the support of a consistent and caring family network to help out in times of trouble. Families are more dispersed now and neighbourhoods are not so close as they might have been when people were more dependent on each other. Religion no longer provides a cohesive community framework as fewer people subscribe to belief in spiritual principles. But whatever the reasons for the breakdown of old community ties, our need for contact and support does not diminish.

If you have got to the stage of knowing that you need some support but not knowing how to get it, you could consider a number of options.

Support groups

There are many groups set up to help people in crisis. Some are focused around a particular difficulty such as alcohol or drug abuse, eating problems, relationship breakdown or depression, while others have a wider purpose, helping people who don't have a particular problem but do want the support of others. Some are facilitated by professional counsellors or social workers; others are run as self-help groups. All of them aim to give you support and contact with people in a similar situation to yourself. Your Community Health Council, local Social Services Department or family doctor can give you information about groups in your area. You can also get help, advice or information from youth clubs, Citizens' Advice Bureaux and public libraries.

Professional counselling

If you are continuing to struggle with serious conflicts and problems you can seek professional counselling or therapy. The British Association for Counselling publishes a register of counsellors and will give you advice on how to choose someone.

When Gerry discovered that her teenage daughter, Sharon, was taking drugs she was very upset. She decided that the best way of dealing with this was to ban her daughter from any after-school activities and to insist that she stayed at home in the evenings and at weekends. Sharon didn't come home from school at all for two days. The plan failed.

Gerry reviewed her plan and decided that improving their relationship, which had obviously become very strained, was her first priority. Her goals included making time to talk and avoiding initiating conflicts over issues which were not important.

Gerry put her new plan into action. When Sharon eventually came home they sat down together and Gerry explained how she was feeling and what her worries were. Sharon did listen and talked a little about her unhappiness about being treated like a child. However this conversation, although it was much better than any contact they had had for a long time, did not solve the problem. Gerry still found herself losing her temper about Sharon's behaviour, and Sharon did not stop taking drugs. Gerry decided to see a professional counsellor because she felt the need of some support for herself; in trying to solve Sharon's problems she realised that she, too, was unhappy.

She went to a counsellor who practised time-limited

therapy – that is, a prescribed number of sessions which was negotiated between the two of them at the beginning of the therapy. In the time they worked together, Gerry came to understand more about how her anxieties were making it hard for her to relate to Sharon. For instance, her need to be a 'perfect mother' meant that her feelings of failure and guilt were very intense. The only way they became bearable was for her to project them on to Sharon, whom she could then blame. Inevitably, their communication usually broke down as Sharon resisted.

As Gerry experienced support from the counsellor and became more knowledgeable about herself she was able to detach herself from Sharon. Communication between mother and daughter became calmer and they were able to explore the drug-taking in a deeper way than before.

In time, Gerry's relationship with her daughter improved. With the counsellor's help Gerry formulated new goals which included making clear decisions about which boundaries were important to stick to and which could be flexible enough to negotiate with Sharon. She also worked on controlling her temper, so that the number of arguments reduced. She explored the anxieties and uncertainties which fuelled her feelings of guilt and realised that some of these were more to do with her than with Sharon and could be resolved by her.

Reviewing your progress regularly will help you feel in control. Whether or not things are going well, you will be in a position to decide what to do next.

EXERCISE

Here are some ways in which you can review your progress.

- *Progress scale.* Draw a line for each of your goals. At one end put the number 1 and at the other number 10. Assuming that 10 indicates complete success, mark where you are along the scale at the moment. What do you need to do to move along to the next number? You can make a wall chart of your goals, moving a pin along the scale as you progress – this is a good way of keeping your goals in constant sight.

- *Skills audit.* No doubt some of your goals involve improving skills you already have or learning new ones. You can keep a check on how you are progressing by listing the skills that would help you achieve your hopes and noting the headway you make with each one.
- *Feedback.* Ask those people who know you whether they have noticed any change in you.

Reflection

When you have completed your review, think about what your next step is going to be. Chapter 10 is the last one, because we are nearly at the end of the counselling process this book describes. You may be at the end your journey of change and ready for life with your new awareness and skills. Or you may want to retrace your steps and reconsider the contract you made. Or perhaps you have decided to work with a professional counsellor. Wherever you are, take a moment to reflect and to value the work you have done.

10

Last Words

Now a whole is that which has a beginning, a middle
and an end.

Aristotle, 384–322 BC

This last chapter is about wholeness. When counsellors and
clients are contemplating the end of their work together,
important issues often arise. For the client this stage may
trigger memories of other endings, some of which may still be
painful to bring to mind. The counsellor's aim will be to feel
that the work has been completed so that the client can use
the experience in his or her future life. Relationships can end
in many ways: someone can die or leave unexpectedly; people
can gradually grow apart from each other; the ending can be
mutual or one person can be left hurt, angry or frightened.

Knowing how to manage endings is important because
they are a natural part of the cycle of life. A good ending is
one which leaves you with the feeling of something
completed – a whole. What are we talking about is not time
prescribed: it can be anything from a very short event – one
meeting, perhaps – to a lifelong relationship. An unsatisfac-
tory end is one which leaves unresolved issues – you may
remember the concept of 'unfinished business' which is so
important in the Gestalt approach to counselling. Even
very early unfinished business can haunt you for the rest of
your life, and one of the purposes of the counselling process
is to help you settle these uncompleted matters.

The importance of spirit

My way of helping you round off the self-counselling process through which this book has guided you is to bring together the three elements which together make your 'whole' – your mind, your body and your spirit. Some of the counselling approaches we have explored tend to reflect our predominantly Western culture by placing more emphasis on mind and body than on spirit. Nevertheless, as I hope you have experienced while working your way through the book, they can be very effective agents of change. But if you are left feeling that something indefinable is missing from your life, perhaps we have not paid enough attention to the spirit which provides a framework of meaning for us.

The word 'spirit' is used in so many ways that it might be useful to stop for a moment and look into some of its meanings. Firstly, it is our spirit which makes us different from everyone else; the sum of all our experience making each one of us uniquely 'I'.

Many people feel that it is also the factor which motivates our search for the meaning of life. Some find that meaning in an existing religious or philosophical structure, others in the order of the natural world, in the study of science or in some other way which satisfies them.

Our spirit can be seen as our collective potential, a source of energy and creativity. It is our spirit which keeps us fighting for what we believe is right even though we may be exhausted; our spirit which shines through the darkest times in our life; our spirit which gives us the sense of being more than a collection of tissue, organs, bones and brain.

The simplest definition might be that our spirit is the most elementary part of our being – our core, which is different from all the elements which make up our personality.

Psychosynthesis: the creation of wholeness

In his book about Psychosynthesis, an approach which sets out to integrate mind, body and spirit, Piero Ferrucci tells the story of a seeker after truth who, after years of searching, was advised to go to a particular cave in which he would find a well which would reveal the truth to him. When the seeker found the well he asked his crucial question, 'Where will I find the truth?' From the depths of the well came the answer, 'Go to the market at the crossroads – there you will find what you are seeking.'

So, of course, he ran to the crossroads. One trader was selling pieces of metal, another pieces of wood and another pieces of wire. The seeker didn't know what to make of this. He went back to the well, only to be told, 'You will understand in the future.' He felt he had no choice but to continue his wandering and searching for truth, full of anger and disappointment. Years went by and the memory of his disappointment at the well faded until one night, while he was walking in the moonlight, he heard the most beautiful music. He followed the sound and came upon a person playing a sitar. The music was marvellous and moved him greatly. He watched the player's skilful fingers dance over the strings, and suddenly he understood. The sitar was made of wires, pieces of metal and wood exactly like those he had seen all those years ago and dismissed as being without significance.

He understood the message of the well to be that we have already been given everything we need; our task is to assemble and use it in the appropriate way. We cannot determine the meaning as long as we see only the separate fragments. Putting the pieces together creates a new entity, whose nature we could not have foreseen by considering only the separate pieces. The intention of this book is to give you a deeper understanding of the separate elements of yourself.

This chapter is concerned with how these elements are balanced to create your whole self.

Roberto Assagioli, the Italian psychiatrist who developed Psychosynthesis, felt that much psychological pain was caused by our distinct inner elements either clashing with or being unaware of each other. He observed that when they merge to create a whole, we experience a release of energy, a sense of wellbeing and a greater depth of meaning in our lives. We have seen how our natural energies can become blocked by our experience of life. The fears and anxieties of childhood; the frustration of our innermost desires; uncertainty about our continuing safety; physical weakness; loss of what we love are just some of the origins of these blocks. Assagioli devised techniques to help people move through these barriers and promote the free flow of the energy which is so necessary for living a full and satisfying life.

The guiding principle of Psychosynthesis is gradual rather than instantaneous change. Assagioli worked on the basis that counselling is a process of education and that our unconscious needs time to assimilate learning. You might, for instance, have had the experience of finding unexpected strength in a crisis; the slow healing of an emotional hurt; inspiration after a long struggle to understand something; sudden realisation of a solution to a puzzle. All these phenomena point to some unconscious impetus which is directed towards balance and completion. This next exercise is an example of one way in which you can increase your awareness of your inner self – your unconscious.

EXERCISE

Take several pieces of paper and coloured pencils or crayons. Give yourself a few moments of quiet before you begin. When you are ready, let your hand draw and watch what images appear on the paper. Develop an attitude of curiosity rather than judgement, and let

---

your hands draw absolutely anything they want. The images may be abstract or figurative; large or small; single or multi-coloured.

While you are observing what you draw, notice also the way in which your hands move – whether they seem certain or tentative; smooth or clumsy; fast or slow, and so on.

When you have finished, study the images. You might even put them away for a while and then look at them.

Look for what the drawing might signify; it has come from you and so it must reflect you in some way. Note down any images or words that come into your mind when you are studying the drawing, even if they don't seem to make a lot of sense.

You can look at the drawing in an analytical way, noting its style, size and colour. For instance, how is the space used? Are the images crowding the paper or squashed into one tiny corner? Is there anything about the images or how you have made them that reflects your self or your life?

You can take the exercise one stage further by converting your emotional response to the images into words. When you have contemplated the drawing for long enough, turn the paper over and write down whatever comes to mind. Again, pretend to be an interested observer of yourself so that you are less likely to censor yourself by writing what you think you *should* write or trying to make sense.

Lisa, on doing this exercise in a group, came up with the image of a bird rising phoenix-like out of flames. In her picture another bird was blocking the way. A small figure stood by watching the two birds. She talked about the picture in this way: 'One bird is trying to stop the other being born. I think I've got both birds in me. The new me is trying to be born but the old me is too frightened to let it happen. I'm the figure watching, too. I can feel the conflict inside every time I want to do something different, and it's as if I'm just watching the battle. I hope the new bird will win, but I'm powerless to help it.'

Some time later she talked to the group about how she had used the picture, which had meant a lot to her, in her everyday life. 'I've been very nervous of speaking up at meetings. Now I realise that I am the one stopping me, and when I want to say something I just go ahead and say it even though I'm still a bit scared. I imagine the new bird flying clear of the flames and spreading its wings. I've learnt to swim, whereas before I wouldn't even get into the water. I've realised that being afraid doesn't have to stop me doing things. I've known the theory of how to change, but somehow I haven't been able to actually do it. The images seemed to come from something deeper – perhaps they represent my spirit which I needed to be in touch with.'

A matter of detachment

To experience ourselves as whole we have to be willing to detach ourselves from our separate parts. It is perhaps because it is so difficult for us to define ourselves other than through what we can see or experience that we closely identify ourselves with these evidences of our existence. If, for instance, I identify myself strongly with a plan that is particularly important to me and it goes wrong, it can feel as if *I* am wrong. A person who identifies totally with the role they play in life – a parent, partner or carer, for example – will feel lost if that role no longer needs to be played. To believe that we are no more than our thoughts, sensations, actions, hopes and fears means that they can control us, limiting our perception of the world. To be in touch with your whole self gives you a greater opportunity to be a

balanced observer of yourself. As you will have noticed
while working through the book, the process of counselling
encourages this kind of objectivity to enable you to evaluate
your situation and make the wisest decisions.

You may feel that this is beginning to sound very cool and
clinical, as if you have to deny your experience and spontaneity. On the contrary, your growing ability to see yourself in
perspective should give you greater choice. You will be able
to distinguish between desire and craving; between opinion
and prejudice; between caution and paranoia; between roles
and masks. Eric Berne, some of whose ideas we used in
earlier chapters, defined spontaneity as the capacity to
choose from a full range of options in feeling, thinking and
behaving. Using this definition, true spontaneity lies in the
ability to choose your response freely to suit the present situation rather than repeating an habitual reaction.

The following Psychosynthesis exercise is an example of
the way you can achieve this kind of overall view of yourself. As in all the meditative exercises, if you are on your
own tape or read through the whole exercise first.

EXERCISE

- Focus your awareness on your body. Notice the
physical sensations of which you are aware. Be
aware, for example, of your contact with the chair
you are sitting on, of your feet on the ground, and
of how your arms are placed.

    Notice areas of tension or discomfort, without
necessarily doing anything to change them. Be
aware of your breathing.

    When you feel you have focused enough on
your body, move on to the next step.

    The Psychosynthesis method for moving on to
the next step is to say to yourself, 'I have a body,
but I am not my body.'

- Now focus on how you are feeling. Your aim is to remain an observer of yourself, so, as you identify the feelings you are experiencing now, just notice them rather than sink into them.

  Ask yourself which are the feelings you experience most often in your life. What are the negative and positive sides of these feelings?

  When you are ready, move on, saying to yourself, 'I have feelings, but I am not my feelings.'
- Now turn your attention to those things you long for in life.

  Take the same neutral attitude as before and review those main desires which are motivating your life. Rather than think about how important any one of them is to you, just consider them side by side, and when you are ready, say to yourself, 'I have longings, but I am not my longings.'
- Now is the time to think about your thoughts.

  Allow each thought to enter your mind and observe it until another takes its place, and so on.

  Don't worry about the right way to do this. Even if you are thinking that you don't have any thoughts, that is what you are thinking and that is what to notice. Finish by telling yourself, 'I have a mind, but I am not my mind.'

This exercise gives you an opportunity to release yourself for a while from the necessity to react to those concerns which are uppermost and dominating your thoughts and feelings. You can continue for one more stage if you wish. This step is planned to afford you an experience of another dimension of yourself – spirit, soul, pure consciousness, inner self, or whatever you might want to call it.

EXERCISE

- Concentrate now on the observer in you, the part
  of yourself who has been watching your sensations,
  feelings, longings and thoughts. This is your inner
  self, who is separate from those things it has been
  observing – more like the essence of the images and
  thoughts you have had. There is no 'right way' to
  do this exercise: just allow yourself to be, without
  putting any effort into getting it correct.

There is no need to worry if you don't get any immediate
'results' from this work. Taking this kind of time to experience ourselves is a rare occurrence for many of us. It is
worth persisting because the rewards are potentially very
beneficial. At the very least, you will have a very effective
stress-reducing technique; the best outcome is that you will
have found a way of accessing your inner self – your spirit.
If you feel this is all getting unrealistic and removed from
everyday matters, be reassured that this awareness need not
take you away from ordinary daily life. On the contrary, it
can be a source of energy and confidence.

Willpower and determination

Another element leading to a satisfying completion of the
counselling work you have done concerns purpose. In the
early stages you made a contract defining the changes you
were hoping to make, and later you set aims and goals to
help you. These strategies were designed to help you find
your direction in life and, even though you have finished
this particular part of the journey, the travelling will
continue.

Many people come into counselling because they want to
be more autonomous – to feel more in control of their lives.

Assagioli placed a great deal of importance on the will, which he saw as an expression of autonomy – the capacity to function freely according to one's own intrinsic nature rather than under the control of external forces. Working through this book will have put you in touch with your own will. Perhaps there were times when it would have been easy to give up, but your willpower pushed you on. This ability to take control of yourself in order to attain your purpose is the strength that counselling can help you develop.

However much change you have been able to achieve at this point, don't expect things to go smoothly for ever. You may find that from time to time you revert to the old behaviour, fall into the traps you have determined to avoid, start the familiar cycle of negative thinking. Bear in mind that learning anything new goes in fits and starts. It is very rare indeed to progress in a continuously upward line; it is much more common to make progress and then fall back, or to reach a plateau and stay on it for what seems like forever. If this happens to you, be kind to yourself. Jenny described her experience in this way. 'It's just like when I was learning to ride. When I started I tried so hard to make the horse do as I wanted. I put a lot of effort into teaching him how to walk and gallop. I thought I had to lift him over all the jumps myself but in time I realised that the horse knew how to walk, trot, gallop and jump perfectly well – my job was to communicate what I wanted and then the horse would do what was necessary. The more I relaxed and accepted the horse, the more we were able to move together. I try to be like that with myself – I know that I can try too hard to succeed. When I relax and accept that I'm doing the best I can and I'm not perfect, I really do feel better. Then, of course, because I feel better I do better!'

Like Jenny, you can take yourself in hand. What is important is that you don't lose sight of your purpose and that your progress is always directed towards that goal. This Psychosynthesis exercise puts you in touch with the

power of your will to keep you on the path you have determined.

EXERCISE

Think about the main purposes in your life at present
and write down a list of the most important ones. You
may have a range of large and small items such as
finishing an essay for college, clearing out the attic,
improving an intimate relationship, starting a family,
learning how to cook and so on. Check over your list to
ensure that you have not included items which are not
real purposes of yours – that is, they might be things
that you feel you ought to do or that other people are
telling you you should do.

Put them in order of importance to you and focus
your awareness on the first item on the list. Close your
eyes and let an image spontaneously arise in your mind
to represent this purpose.

Keeping your eyes closed, imagine this image placed
high on a hill in front of you. You can see the path up
to the image and you begin walking up it.

On both sides of you, while you are walking, you can
hear voices telling you of all the difficulties, and in
front of you appear various barriers to your progress.

None of these voices or barriers can take you off the
path which you can continue climbing. You can listen
to the voices and know that, however logical or right
they believe they are, they cannot divert you from your
purpose. See yourself surmount each barrier. See if
you can understand what motivation lies behind each
of these diversions; you can stop, explore and hold a
dialogue with any of them – but then move on.

When you reach the top, stay with the image of your
purpose for a while and enjoy having reached it.
Experience how it feels to have got to this point.

> When you are ready, open your eyes and write about, draw or paint this experience.
>
> Repeat the exercise as often as you like for your different purposes. It is fruitful whenever you feel you have lost your way on the journey to change.

Trust you!

One of the results of a successful counselling experience is that you will trust yourself more. This trust will develop through your greater understanding and acceptance of your whole self – mind, body and spirit. You may find that you are more aware of your intuition – that voice which seems to come more from our feelings than from our intellect. You could say that our intuition is the voice of our spirit, with as much reason to be taken into account as the voice of our mind. Many of us are in the habit of ignoring or distrusting our intuition because we live in a culture which places more value on the intellect than on feelings. I am not suggesting that we go the other way and ignore reason – only that we give each part of ourselves equal weight so that when we make a decision it is on the basis of our whole self.

To trust your intuition means tuning into your inner feelings, your hunches. Try checking in regularly to your intuition, two or three times a day. This just means taking a moment to relax and listening in to yourself. Experiment with asking for help when you need it and waiting for images, words or feelings to come into your mind. Practise listening to these messages, because they may hold important information for you. The following meditation exercise gives you a way to begin doing this.

EXERCISE

Sit or lie in a comfortable position in a quiet place. Close your eyes and relax. Take several slow, deep breaths, relaxing your body more with each one. Let your thoughts drift in and out of your mind without focusing on any particular one.

Focus your attention in the area of your stomach or solar plexus, which is the area from which our feelings seem to arise – hence the term 'gut feelings'!

Imagine that you have a source of wisdom there. Give this source an image if you wish – maybe a wise person, animal or symbol. Communicate silently with this source, making requests, asking questions, inviting perceptions. You might ask, for instance, 'Intuition, tell me what I could do at this point.'

Any response you get will be coming from the collected wisdom you have gathered throughout your life. We learn something from every experience, but we can't keep that learning in our conscious mind all the time. Just because we are not thinking about it doesn't mean it has disappeared – you would be surprised at how much you knew if it was all in your conscious mind. There is information, too, that we are taking in all the time with all our senses. For instance, people register their feelings with tiny body movements and changes in breathing which we see and hear even if we don't consciously record the fact. This is the information that feeds those feelings we have about people, places or events for which we can't give a reason.

If you don't experience any response, don't worry about it. Just continue with your everyday life. You may find that an answer does come, perhaps later, in the form of a feeling or a new thought. You might be attracted to a particular book, meet a person or go to a place from which you get an insight. You may have a dream which is significant, or you may wake up from your sleep with a solution in mind.

Whatever form your intuition takes, don't ignore it. It is likely to be your true response to your situation. You may decide for good reasons not to act on it, just as you might not act on advice given to you by any other person. Taking it into account just means treating yourself as equally important as others. Many people find that they feel more alive and powerful when they act on their intuition and that opportunities open up for them. If you are not sure, be guided by how right it feels to act on these hunches. If it doesn't feel right, check whether you are responding to your genuine intuition or to those other forces which motivate us such as our conscience, old beliefs, other people's opinions, doubts and anxieties, and so on.

One to one

This book has been about you undertaking some change in your self or your life. To return to the analogy we have used from time to time, we are at the last stop of this particular part of the journey. It's time to move on to the next stage. Perhaps you have been able to shed some old luggage which was weighing you down unnecessarily; you may have new learning and understanding to take with you into the future.

Throughout the book we have used the ideas of people who have been instrumental in fashioning contemporary methods of counselling. We will end with Carl Rogers, whose work in this field has been highly influential. In writing about the purposes of counselling and therapy he says, 'The experience to which I am referring is a central process or central aspect of psychotherapy. It is the experience of becoming a more autonomous, more spontaneous, more confident person. It is the experience of freedom to be oneself.'

It is this freedom which I hope you will experience as a result of working through this book. I wish you well.

References and Further Reading

Bandler, Richard, and John Grinder: *Frogs into Princes*, Real People Press (1979)

Bandler, Richard, and John Grinder: *The Structure of Magic (part 1)*; Science and Behavior Books, Palo Alto, California (1975)

Berne, Eric: *Principles of Group Treatment*, Grove Press, New York (1966)

Berne, Eric: *What Do You Say After You Say Hello?*, Grove Press, New York (1966)

Egan, Gerard: *The Skilled Helper*, Brooks/Cole Publishing Co. (1982)

Ellis, Albert: *Humanistic Psychotherapy: The Rational-Emotive Approach*, McGraw Hill, New York (1974)

Ernst, Sheila, and Lucy Goodison: *In Our Own Hands*, The Women's Press (1984)

Ferrucci, Piero: *What We May Be*, Turnstone Press (1982)

Friel, John, and Linda Friel: *Adult Children. The Secrets of Dysfunctional Families*, Health Communications Inc. (1988)

Goulding, Robert, and Mary Goulding: 'Injunctions, Decisions and Redecisions' *Transactional Analysis Journal*, 6, 1, 1976, 41–8

Houston, Gaie: *The Relative-Sized Red Book of Gestalt*, The Rochester Foundation (1982)

Jackins, Harvey, *The Upward Trend*, Rational Island Publishers, Seattle (1978)

Kubler-Ross, Elisabeth: *Death: The Final Stage of Growth*, Prentice-Hall Inc. (1975)

Leming, Michael R., and George E. Dickinson: *Understanding Dying, Death and Bereavement*, Holt, Rinehart & Winston (1985)

Macaskill, Norman D. and Ann Macaskill: 'Cognitive Therapy for Depression: The Efficacy of Minimal Intervention Programmes', *Bulletin of the Association of Behavioural Cognitive Psychotherapy* (1991, Vol. X, pp. 13–20)

Macaskill, Norman D. and Anne Macaskill: 'Cognitive Therapy for Depression: A Selective Review of Self-Help Materials', *Bulletin of the Association of Behavioural Cognitive Psychotherapy* (1992, Vol. XII, pp. 5–13)

Nelson-Jones, Richard: *The Theory and Practice of Counselling Psychology*, Holt, Rinehart & Winston (1983)

Parkes, Colin Murray: *Bereavement; Studies of Grief in Adult Life*, Penguin (1988)

Peck, Connie: *Controlling Chronic Pain*, Fontana (1985)

Perls, F., *Gestalt Therapy Verbatim*, Real People Press (1969)

Perls, F., R. Hefferline and P. Goodman: *Gestalt Therapy*, Penguin Books (1976)

Rogers, Carl R. and Barry Stevens: *Person to Person*, Souvenir Press (1967)

Saraganian, Peter (ed.): *Exercise Psychology: The Influence of Physical Exercise on Psychological Processes*, John Wiley & Sons (1993)

Satir, Virginia: *Conjoint Family Therapy*; Science and Behavior Books, Palo Alto, California (1967)

Schutz, W.C.: *The Interpersonal Underworld*, Science and Behavior Books, Palo Alto, California (1967)

Sheehy, Gail: *Passages*, E.P. Dutton, New York (1974)

Skinner, B.F.: *Science and Human Behaviour*, Free Press, New York (1953)

Southgate, John, and Rosemary Randall, *The Barefoot Psychoanalyst*, Association of Karen Horney Psychoanalytic Counsellors, London (1978)

Spitz, René: 'Hospitalism: Genesis of Psychiatric Conditions in Early Childhood', *Psychoanalytic Studies of the Child* (1, 1945, pp. 53–74)

Stewart, Ian and Vann Joines: *TA Today*, Lifespace Publishing (1987)

Useful Addresses

British Association for Counselling, 1 Regent Place, Rugby, Warwickshire, CV21 2PJ (Information: 01788 578328).
Runs an information office and publishes directories describing counselling services and training in counselling.

British Association of Psychotherapists, 37 Mapesbury Road, London NW2 4HJ (0181 452 9823).
A professional organisation of psychotherapists offering training and a prompt assessment and referral system for children, adolescents and adults requiring psychotherapy.

Centre for Stress Management, 156 Westcombe Hill, London SE3 7DH (0181 293 4114).
Offers counselling, therapy and supervision as well as in-house courses, seminars and workshops; staff counselling in organisations and a programme of short courses.

Gestalt Centre, 60 Bunhill Row, London EC1.
Offers training workshops, groups, supervision, individual or couples counselling and therapy.

Guild of Psychotherapists, 149 Faraday Road, London SW19 8PA (0181 540 4454).
Central referral service to psychotherapists in all areas.

Metanoia, 13 North Common Road, Ealing, London W5 2QB (0181 579 2505).
Training in a number of counselling and psychotherapy approaches.

MIND, Fitzwilliam House, 10 St Mary Axe, London EC3A 8NA (0171 372 4940).
Professional training; counselling and psychotherapy of all kinds available to groups and individuals.

Psychosynthesis & Education Trust, 92–4 Tooley Street, London SE1 2TH (0171 403 2100).
Professional training, experiential self-development workshops and counselling and psychotherapy service.

WPF Counselling, 23 Kensington Square, London W8 5HN (0171 937 6956).
Provides individual and group counselling as well as professional training.

CHOOSING A COUNSELLOR

Working through this book may have encouraged you to take up the option of employing a professional counsellor to help you work through issues which seem too big to work through on your own.

Some counsellors work for organisations; others have freelance private practices. Some specialise in particular problems such as eating disorders or addiction; others work with specific groups like adolescents, families or couples. Finding the right person for you may take time but it is worth shopping around.

The final judge of whether a counsellor is right for you can only be yourself and you must trust your own instincts. Talk to the counsellor first and then ask yourself some questions. For instance, would you feel comfortable telling this person intimate details of your life? Do you feel safe with them? Do you like their manner towards you?

The British Association for Counselling (BAC) publishes a *Counselling and Psychotherapy Resources Directory* in which counsellors who abide by a reputable code of ethics and practice are listed, together with voluntary organisations and self-help groups. The BAC can also provide a list of counsellors or organisations available in your locality.

Some voluntary or charitable organisations offer free counselling or ask only for a donation towards their costs. These include the Alcohol Counselling Service, RELATE and Cruse Bereavement. Specialist counselling is offered by agencies affiliated to national organisations like Standing Conference on Drug Abuse (SCODA). There are also local counselling services, details of which are usually obtainable from your local library or information office.

Some counselling is available on the National Health Service. This will usually require a referral from your GP, although some hospital Clinical Psychology Departments will take self referrals. There is an increasing trend for counsellors to be part of the General Practice team so it is worth asking if your doctor can refer you to a counsellor.

Index

Index